BrightRED Study Guide

Curriculum for Excellence

N4

COMPUTING SCIENCE

Alan Williams

First published in 2015 by:
Bright Red Publishing Ltd
1 Torphichen Street
Edinburgh
EH3 8HX

A CIP record for this book is available from the British Library

ISBN 978-1-906736-48-4

With thanks to:
PDQ Digital Media Solutions Ltd, Bungay (layout and illustrations), Clodagh Burke (copy-edit)

Cover design and series book design by Caleb Rutherford – e i d e t i c

Acknowledgements
Every effort has been made to seek all copyright holders. If any have been overlooked, then Bright Red Publishing will be delighted to make the necessary arrangements.

Permission has been sought from all relevant copyright holders and Bright Red Publishing are grateful for the use of the following:

CandyBox Images/Shutterstock.com (p 4); jaylopez/freeimages.com (p 6); Scratch is developed by the Lifelong Kindergarten Group at the MIT Media Lab. See http://scratch.mit.edu (CC BY-SA 2.0)3 (pp 8, 11, 12, 13, 18, 20, 22, 88); Windows 8 Release Preview Start Screen used with permission from Microsoft (p 9); cobrasoft/freeimages.com (p 10); Stephen Coburn/Shutterstock.com (p 12); giel/freeimages.com (p 13); Konstantin Chagin/Shutterstock.com (p 14); Johnragai-Moment Catcher (CC BY 2.0)1 (p 16); Alan Light (CC BY 2.0)1 (p 16); scanrail/iStock.com (p 16); lanych/iStock.com (p 17); Caleb Rutherford e i d e t i c (p 18); René (and then some) (CC BY 2.0)1 (p 18); AlexRaths/iStock.com (p 19); ollycb/freeimages.com (p 20); aga-grafik/freeimages.com (p 22); Daniilantiq/iStock.com (p 23); sergign/Shutterstock.com (p 24); Devonyu/iStock.com (p 25); NBNMick/freeimages.com (p 26); GiniMiniGi/freeimages.com (p 27); Garry Knight (CC BY 2.0)1 (p 28); nensuria/iStock.com (p 29); BBC News & Current Affairs/Getty Images (p 30); Caleb Rutherford e i d e t i c (p 30); Caleb Rutherford e i d e t i c (p 30); marinart1/Shutterstock.com (p 33); leaf/iStock.com (p 33); Caleb Rutherford - e i d e t i c (p 34); pawel_231/freeimages.com (p 35); Gordon Tarpley (CC BY 2.0)1 (p 36); Michal Zacharzewski/freeimages.com (p 37); Caleb Rutherford e i d e t i c (p 37); Sean MacEntee (CC BY 2.0)1 (p 38); versevend/iStock.com (p 38); c8501089/iStock.com (p 39); Pakmor/Shutterstock.com (p 40); Michal Zacharzewski/freeimages.com (p 40); Caleb Rutherford - e i d e t i c (p 41); Jezper/Shutterstock.com (p 42); bumihills/Shutterstock.com (p 42); Franck-Boston/iStock.com (p 42); Caleb Rutherford e i d e t i c (p 43); Filip Krstic/Shutterstock.com (p 44); Caleb Rutherford e i d e t i c (p 44); Caleb Rutherford e i d e t i c (p 45); Tambako The Jaguar (CC BY-ND 2.0)2 (p 46); Reddiplomat/iStock.com (p 46); dsa046/iStock.com (p 46); The Dress Up Place (CC BY-SA 2.0)3 (p 47); Simply Swim UK (CC BY-SA 2.0)3 (p 47); fh.mum1 (CC BY 2.0)1 (p 48); Caleb Rutherford - e i d e t i c (p 49); ArtMarie/iStock.com (p 50); Jennifer C. (CC BY 2.0)1 (p 51); AndreyPopov/iStock.com (p 51); Caleb Rutherford e i d e t i c (p 52); fotek/iStock.com (p 53); reynermedia (CC BY 2.0)1 (p 54); Mervana/iStock.com (p 55); AnikaSalsera/iStock.com (p 56); scanrail/iStock.com (p 56); BrightRED (p 56); tetmc/iStock.com (p 58); Qwasyx/iStock.com (p 59); VikaSuh/iStock.com (p 60); gehringj/iStock.com (p 62); Caleb Rutherford e i d e t i c (p 63); Davide Guglielmo/freeimages.com, Caleb Rutherford e i d e t i c (p 64); Gabriela Ruellan/freeimages.com (p 64); Zardinax/iStock.com (p 68); shironosov/iStock.com (p 70); Caleb Rutherford e i d e t i c (p 71); Caleb Rutherford e i d e t i c (p 77); monkeybusinessimages/iStock.com (p 78); Romangorielov/Dreamstime.com (p 78); Caleb Rutherford e i d e t i c (p 79); Caleb Rutherford e i d e t i c (p 81); lisegagne/iStock (p 83); Image of a QuickBuilder Bar from Serif WebPlus © Serif (Europe) Ltd. (p 85); Website image © Ticketmaster UK Ltd (p 86); gemphoto/Shutterstock.com (p 87); Allie_Caulfield (CC BY 2.0)1 (pp 84 & 85); Jerome Bon (CC BY 2.0)1 (pp 84 & 85).

(CC BY 2.0)1   http://creativecommons.org/licenses/by/2.0/

(CC BY-ND 2.0)2   http://creativecommons.org/licenses/by-nd/2.0/

(CC BY-SA 2.0)3   http://creativecommons.org/licenses/by-sa/2.0/

Printed and bound in the UK by Ashford Colour Press Ltd.

CONTENTS

NATIONAL 4 COURSE

OUTLINE OF THE COURSE 4

SOFTWARE DESIGN AND DEVELOPMENT

Binary Representations 6

Data Types and Structures 8

Expressions and Arithmetic Operators 10

Sequencing, Selection and Iteration 12

Design Notations 14

Testing and Documenting Solutions 16

Questions 1 18

Questions 2 20

Questions 3 22

Learning Outcomes and Unit Assessment 24

Practice Learning Outcome 1 26

Practice Learning Outcome 2 28

Practice Learning Outcome 3 30

INFORMATION SYSTEM DESIGN AND DEVELOPMENT

Databases 32

Websites 34

Media Types 36

Purpose, Features, Functionality and Users 38

Technical Implementation (Hardware, Software, Storage, Connectivity) 40

Security Risks 42

Impact of IT on the Environment and Society 44

Questions 1 46

Questions 2 48

Questions 3 50

Learning Outcomes and Unit Assessment 52

Practice Learning Outcome 1 54

Practice Learning Outcome 2 56

THE ASSIGNMENT

Outline of the Assignment 58

Practice Assignment Part A 60

Practice Assignment Part B 62

Practice Assignment Documentation 64

ANSWERS AND SOLUTIONS

Software Design and Development: Answers 1 66

Software Design and Development: Answers 2 68

Software Design and Development: Answers 3 70

Software Design and Development: Solution to Practice Learning Outcome 1 72

Software Design and Development: Solution to Practice Learning Outcome 2 74

Software Design and Development: Solution to Practice Learning Outcome 3 76

Information System Design and Development: Answers 1 78

Information System Design and Development: Answers 2 80

Information System Design and Development: Answers 3 82

Information System Design and Development: Solution to Practice Learning Outcome 1 84

Information System Design and Development: Solution to Practice Learning Outcome 2 86

The Assignment: Solution to Practice Assignment Part A 88

The Assignment: Solution to Practice Assignment Part B 90

The Assignment: Solution to Practice Assignment Documentation 92

Solutions to Tasks and Course Ideas 94

GLOSSARY 95

NATIONAL 4 COURSE

OUTLINE OF THE COURSE

INTRODUCTION

The National 4 Computing Science course is made up of the three units shown in the table below.

Unlike the National 5 course there is no external exam for the National 4 course. The assessment for this course is a combination of unit assessments and a practical course assignment.

Unit	Assessment
Software Design and Development	Unit assessment
Information System Design and Development	Unit assessment
Added Value Unit	Course assignment

Unit Assessments

The Software Design and Development unit and the Information System Design and Development unit involve theory and practical work. To pass each of these units you are required to complete a number of theory and practical unit assessment tasks.

Course Assignment

The Added Value unit involves a course assignment that takes place towards the end of the course. It takes the form of a practical project that will ask you to apply the skills that you have learned in the other two units.

COURSE CONTENT

The tables below give a summary of the content of the National 4 course.

Software Design and Development

Software Design and Development	
Low-level operations and computer architecture	Use of binary to represent positive integers, characters and instructions (machine code) Units of storage (bit, byte, Kb, Mb, Gb, Tb, Pb)
Data types and structures	String and Integer variables Graphical object
Expressions and arithmetic operations	Expressions to assign values to variables Expressions to return values using arithmetic operations (+, -, *, /, ^)
Sequence, selection and iteration	Execution of instructions in sequence demonstrating input – process – output Selection constructs including simple conditional statements (IF) Iteration using fixed and conditional loops
Testing and documenting solutions	Normal, extreme and exceptional test data Readability of code (internal commentary, meaningful variable names)
Design notations	Graphical design notation to illustrate selection and iteration Other contemporary design notations

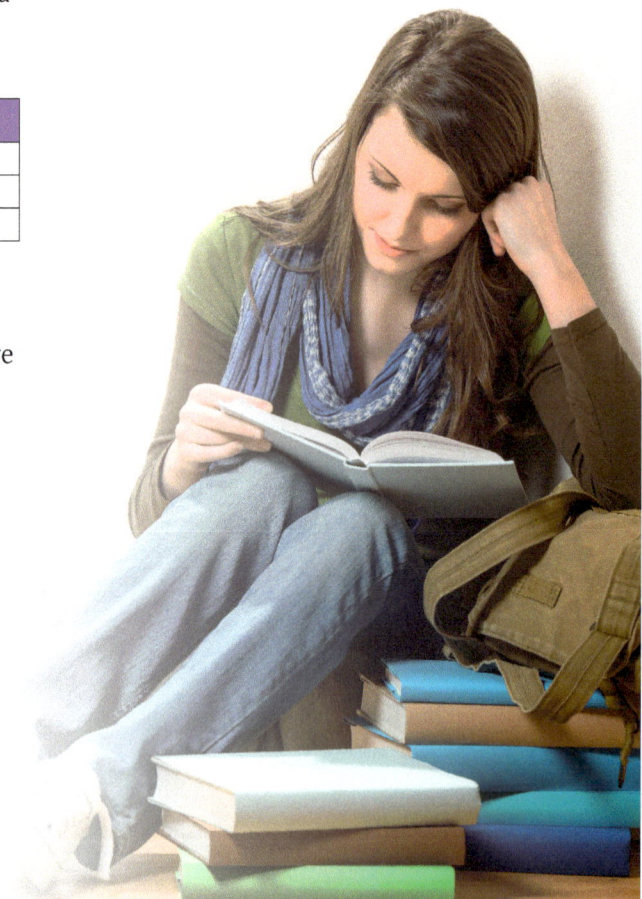

Information System Design and Development

Information System Design and Development			
Databases	Database structure: field, record, file Field types (text, numbers, date, time, graphics, calculated) Database operations (search, sort)		
Websites	Website, page, URL, Hyperlink		
Media types	Sound, graphics, video, text		
Purpose, features, functionality and users	Description of the purpose of an application Descriptions of the main features and functionality Users: expert, novice, age-range		
Technical Implementation (Hardware, software, storage, connectivity)	Hardware -input and output devices -processor clock speed (Hz) -memory (RAM, ROM) Operating system	Storage devices -built-in, external, portable -magnetic, optical -capacity, speed -rewritable, read-only	Connectivity -stand-alone or networked -LAN/internet -wired/wireless
Security risks	Viruses, worms, Trojans, hacking		
Impact of IT on the environment and society	Use of energy and resources and carbon footprint Impact on people in society		

COURSE ASSIGNMENT

The course assignment is not a small task that can be completed in a couple of periods but a lengthy project that will probably require a couple of months work. It involves the analysis, design and implementation of a solution to a problem. The practical solution must then be thoroughly tested with suitably chosen sets of test data and finally the solution is evaluated.

Your solution is documented in a report which must include evidence of the stages of development of the project. For example there should be a sketch of the design of the program interface, screenshots of test runs, a listing of the program code, and so on.

A much more detailed description of the course assignment is found in the last chapter of this book.

PURPOSE OF THIS BOOK

The purpose of this book is to improve your chances of success in this course by preparing you for the unit assessments and the course assignment.

The theory content of this course is covered in detail and questions and answers are included to test your understanding.

To prepare you for the assessments there are practice unit assessment tasks and their solutions and also a practice course assignment project and its solution.

YOUR PROGRESS

Your teacher will have a record of how you are progressing through this course in terms of the unit assessments and the course assignment. Ask your teacher from time to time how you are doing and what you still have left to do to complete these tasks.

JUST A WEE NOTE

The course assignment is marked as a pass or a fail by your teacher. You do not need to attain a certain percentage mark but simply to provide evidence that you have achieved the requirements of each stage of the task.

DON'T FORGET

To successfully complete this course you need to pass the unit assessments for the Software Design and Development and the Information System Design and Development units. In addition you must also pass an assignment task which is a practical task that is based upon these two units.

THINGS TO DO AND THINK ABOUT

The aim of the National 4 Course is summarised by the points given below:

- To develop knowledge and understanding of important concepts and processes in computing science.
- To apply your skills and knowledge in analysing, designing, implementing and evaluating a range of digital solutions.
- To describe and explain computing concepts clearly using appropriate terms.
- To develop an understanding of the role and impact of computing science on the environment and society.

SOFTWARE DESIGN AND DEVELOPMENT

BINARY REPRESENTATIONS

BINARY NUMBERS

A computer uses electric charges set to two different values (ON or OFF) to store data and program instructions. Just like an electric kettle, the charge can be represented by a 1 for ON and a 0 for OFF.

ON · OFF

The data stored on a computer can be represented by binary numbers which are made up of the two digits 1 and 0. Numbers, text and program instructions are represented on a computer system in codes using patterns of 1s and 0s.

JUST A WEE NOTE

It is quite common for students to mistake the last binary unit in a number (the one on the right) as a group of two instead of a unit. For example the binary number 1101 = 8 + 4 + 1 = 13 and not 16 + 8 + 2 =26.

POSITIVE NUMBERS

Positive whole numbers are represented in a computer system in the binary number system. The binary number system uses units of twos, fours, eights, sixteens, and so on. to represent a number instead of the units of tens, hundreds, thousands, and so on. used in the decimal system.

JUST A WEE NOTE

The answer can be checked by converting it back into the original decimal number as shown in the previous example.

Changing Binary Numbers to Decimal

This example shows how to convert the binary number 10111001 to decimal.

EXAMPLE

```
128 64 32 16  8  4  2  1
 1  0  1  1  1  0  0  1 = 128 + 32 + 16 + 8 + 1 = 185.
```

Changing Decimal Numbers to Binary

This example shows how to convert the number 147 to binary.

EXAMPLE

The number 147 is repeatedly divided by 2 until it is equal to 0.

Write down the remainders at each step of division. The remainders (reading from bottom to top) give the binary number.

The answer = 10010011.

Write down the remainder after each division.

2	147	
2	73	R 1
2	36	R 1
2	18	R 0
2	9	R 0
2	4	R 1
2	2	R 0
2	1	R 0
	0	R 1

Keep dividing until you get to zero.

VIDEO LINK

Watch the tutorial 'How to Convert a Binary Number to a Decimal Number' at http://www.youtube.com/watch?v=e5EmvJfSz7A

TASK   Crossnumber

Copy and complete the crossnumber puzzle using binary numbers.
The first answer has been done for you. The solution can be found on p94.

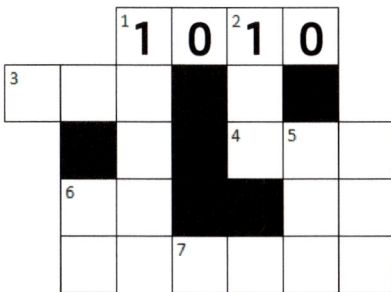

The solution can be found on p94.

Across
1   You have this number of fingers on two hands.
3   You start primary school at this age.
4   A hexagon has this number of sides.
6   The number of bears in the children's story.
7   A dozen.

Down
1   An unlucky number.
2   A lucky number.
5   There is this number of playing card suits.
6   A couple.

CHARACTERS

Text is stored on a computer by representing each individual character as a unique binary code. The characters include letters (upper and lower case), numeric digits (0 to 9), punctuation marks (?, &, !, £, and so on) and mathematical operations (+, -, *, /, and so on).

ASCII (American Standard Code for Information Interchange)

ASCII is a common system for representing text that uses an 8 bit (1 byte) code for each character. For example, the letter E is stored as 01000101 (or 69 in decimal).

UNITS

The following units of storage are used to represent the size of files and the capacity of storage devices on computer systems:

MACHINE CODE

Machine code is the computer's own programming language which uses binary codes to represent the program instructions and data.

Machine code programs are very difficult for humans to write and it is easy to make mistakes since all instructions are made up of patterns of 1s and 0s. High level languages were developed to make it easier and quicker to write programs.

A Bit is a binary digit	(1 or 0)
A Byte is a group of 8 bits.	(eg. 10111011)
A Kilobyte (Kb) is 1,024 bytes.	(2^{10} bytes)
A Megabyte (Mb) is 1,024 kilobytes = 1,048,576 bytes.	(2^{20} bytes)
A Gigabyte (Gb) is 1,024 megabytes = 1,073,741,824 bytes.	(2^{30} bytes)
A Terabyte (Tb) is 1,024 gigabytes = 1,099,511,627,776 bytes.	(2^{40} bytes)
A Petabyte (Pb) is 1,024 terabytes = 1,125,899,906,842,624 bytes.	(2^{50} bytes)

COURSE IDEA

A word processing program uses binary numbers to store numbers, characters and the program instructions. For example the wordcount would be stored as a binary number, the document text would be stored using binary codes for each character and the program itself is stored in binary numbers to represent the machine code instructions.

Describe three examples of where binary codes would be used by a computer program playing the game hangman.

SUMMARY

Binary numbers are used in a computer system to represent positive integers, characters and instructions (machine code).
Units of storage in increasing order of size are bit, byte, Kb, Mb, Gb, Tb and Pb.

THINGS TO DO AND THINK ABOUT

At one time floppy discs were used to make copies of data on a computer system. A floppy disc had a capacity of 1.4 Mb. Use a search engine to find the capacity in Gb of any USB memory stick. How many times more data can it store than a floppy disc?

DATA TYPES AND STRUCTURES

VARIABLES

Variables are used in programs to store items of data such as a surname, age, exam mark, and so on, that are entered by the user or are the result of a calculation.

A variable is a label given to an item of data so that program instructions can identify them. It is easier to understand programs that use meaningful names for variables such as Surname, Age and Passes and not S, A and P or even worse X, Y and Z.

Most programming languages require the variables used in a program to be declared before they are used.

This makes the program easier to understand by clearly stating which variables are used by the program and also allows the program to set memory aside to store the variables. In a large commercial program the amount of data stored in variables can be several Megabytes.

For example in the programming language Scratch the variables are created by selecting the orange "Variables" TAB and then clicking on the "Make a Variable" button.

DATA TYPES

A variable such as Surname will hold a piece of text whereas a variable called Age will hold a number. For this reason different **data types** are needed to store different kinds of data in programs.

Integers

The INTEGER data type is used for a variable that is storing a positive or negative whole number.

e.g. 18, -40, 66, 0, -555, 65,536, and so on.

An INTEGER data type could be used in a program to store an age, the number of people on a bus, the number of a ball in the national lottery, and so on.

String

The STRING data type is used for a variable that is storing an item of text.

eg. "Violin", "Himalayas", Yes", "Don't walk", "F", and so on.

A STRING data type could be used in a program to store a surname, town, colour, and so on.

Declaring Variables

Some programming languages use a DIM statement to declare variables. DIM stands for dimension.

DIM Age As INTEGER

DIM Planet As STRING

DIM GoalsScored As INTEGER

DIM Town As STRING

DON'T FORGET

The name given to a variable must not contain any spaces or start with a number. For example ExamMark is OK but Exam Mark or 1Mark are not allowed.

EXAMPLE

The golf game shown below needs to store program variables.

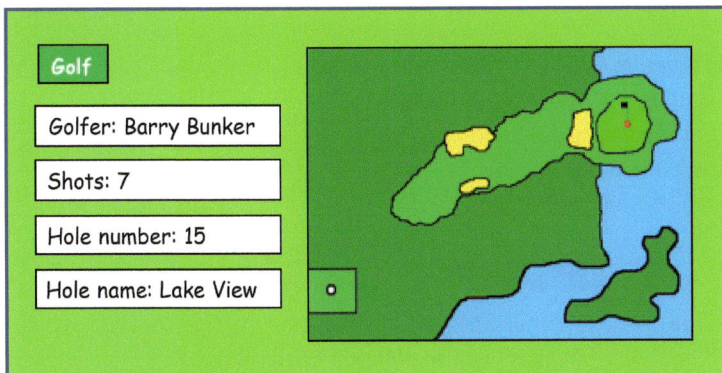

JUST A WEE NOTE

The programming language Scratch does not let the programmer define different data types. You simply create variables with a suitable name and the program will take care of what type of data the variable is storing.

The name of the golfer is stored in a variable which would be a STRING data type since it is storing someone's name which is a piece of text.

The number of shots taken at a hole is a variable which would be stored in an INTEGER data type since it is storing small whole numbers such as 3, 4, 5, 6, and so on.

The number of the hole is variable which would be stored in an INTEGER data type since it is storing a whole number from 1 to 18.

The name of the hole is variable which would be stored in a STRING data type since it is storing the name of the hole which is a piece of text.

Graphical Objects

Software can be made more attractive and colourful with the use of suitable images. The images can be imported into the interface from a graphic file that has already been created or produced within the program as in languages such as Scratch.

COURSE IDEA

Select an App game that you play on your phone. The program will store items of data in variables.

Write down as many examples of STRING and INTEGER data types that the App uses.

Swap with other students in your class and do the same task for their Apps.

SUMMARY

Programming languages store data in variables. The variables must be declared before they are used, at which point they are given a data type. For this course you need to know only two data types: STRING and INTEGER.

THINGS TO DO AND THINK ABOUT

For the main programming language that you use in your school make sure that you know how to declare STRING and INTEGER data types. Always think carefully about which data type to use for your program variables.

EXPRESSIONS AND ARITHMETIC OPERATORS

EXPRESSIONS

Variables are used in programs to store and process items of data. Expressions are used to assign a value to a variable. For a variable which is an Integer data type the value assigned to the variable can either be a number or the result of a calculation using other variables. For a variable which is a String data type the variable can be assigned an item of text or the result of processing other variables which are storing text.

EXAMPLE

The following expression assigns the constant value 20 to the Discount variable.

SET Discount TO 20

EXAMPLE

The following expression assigns the item of text "Dagger" to the Weapon variable.

SET Weapon TO "Dagger"

EXAMPLE

The following expression calculates the area of a rectangle from the length and breadth and assigns it to the Area variable.

SET Area TO Length * Breadth

EXAMPLE

The following expression joins a first name and a space and a surname together and assigns it to the Fullname variable.

SET Fullname TO Firstname & " " & Surname

ARITHMETIC OPERATIONS (+, - *, /, ^)

Programming languages perform addition, subtraction, multiplication, division and powers operations. These operations are represented by the symbols shown in the table shown below. The symbols for these operations can vary for different programming languages but the ones used in the table are most commonly used and are the ones that you should know for this course. The programming languages Visual Basic, Python and Scratch all use these symbols but note that Python uses "**" instead of "^" for powers.

Operation	Symbol
Add	+
Subtract	-
Multiply	*
Divide	/
Power	^

JUST A WEE NOTE

Make sure that you use the symbols "*" and "/" to perform multiplication and division in computer programs and not "x" and "÷".

The following examples illustrate some uses of these operations:

EXAMPLE

This instruction calculates the number of pupils in a class.

SET ClassSize TO Boys + Girls

EXAMPLE

This instruction calculates an employee's net pay after tax is taken off the gross pay.

SET NetPay TO GrossPay - Tax

EXAMPLE

This instruction calculates the share of the jackpot that the winners of the national lottery receive.

SET Share TO Jackpot / NumberofWinners

EXAMPLE

This instruction calculates the area of a circle from the radius.

SET Area TO 3.14 * Radius ^ 2

set Time to 0

set Lives to 3

set Points to Points + 10

set Final Score to Score - Penalties

set Dollars to Pounds * Exchange Rate

set Share to Jackpot / Number of Winners

set Total Points to Start Points + Win Points * Number of Wins

Scratch

Shown to the left are some examples from Scratch where variables are assigned the value of an expression using the SET script which is found on the Variables tab and the arithmetic operations which are found on the Operators tab.

Visual Basic

Shown below are some examples from Visual Basic where variables are assigned the value of an expression.

Age = 16

Colour = "Blue"

Area = Length * Breadth

COURSE IDEA

The Scratch programming language has a string operation called Join that is found in the Operators tab. Create a Scratch program with two variables to store the first name and surname of the user. Then use the Join operator to combine strings to make interesting phrases.

Enter the script shown below and then make up some more complex phrases using the First name and Surname variables. Try and make up phrases such as:

"Hello Tom, how are you today?"

"Tom Anderson is a nice name."

"I was at school with someone called Tom Anderson."

when ⚑ clicked

ask What's your name? and wait

set First name to answer

ask What's your surname? and wait

set Surname to answer

say join Hello First name for 2 secs

SUMMARY

Expressions use arithmetic operations (+, -. *, /,) to assign values to variables. You will need to use expressions in your practical programming tasks for unit assessment and course assessment. Make sure that you know the format of the instruction that use expressions to assign values to variables in the programming languages that you use.

THINGS TO DO AND THINK ABOUT

For a program that you have written in your school, print out the program code and highlight any instructions that use expressions to assign values to variables. Try to do this for two different programing languages such as Visual Basic and Scratch.

ONLINE

This online calculator works out the area of a circle from the radius: http://www.calculateme.com/cArea/AreaOfCircle.htm. Can you find another example of an arithmetic operation online?

DON'T FORGET

It is more efficient to use the power symbol than to multiply a variable by itself. For example Length ^ 3 is more efficient than Length * Length * Length.

SEQUENCING, SELECTION AND ITERATION

INTRODUCTION

Programs are made up of a set of instructions that are executed to solve a problem. The order in which the instructions are executed are controlled by three basic programming constructs. These are called sequence, selection and iteration.

SEQUENCE

Sequencing is when the program executes a list of instructions one after another.

JUST A WEE NOTE

This program is an example of Input-Process-Output, where a program enters data, performs a calculation and then displays the result of the calculation. This is essentially how all programs work.

EXAMPLE

The following program is an example of sequencing. It enters the sides of a rectangle and then calculates and displays the area and perimeter of the rectangle. The instructions in this program are executed in sequence one after the other. There is no repetition of instructions or branching within the program.

```
when [flag] clicked
set Length to 0
set Breadth to 0
set Area to 0
set Perimeter to 0
ask Please enter the length of rectangle and wait
set Length to answer
ask Please enter the breadth of rectangle and wait
set Breadth to answer
set Area to (Length * Breadth)
set Perimeter to (2 * Length + 2 * Breadth)
say join The area of the rectangle is Area for 2 secs
say join The perimeter of the rectangle is Perimeter for 2 secs
```

Set up variables with a value of zero

Enter the length and breadth

Calculate the area and perimeter

Display the results

SELECTION

Computer programs are required to make decisions and execute different sets of instructions depending on the value of variables. For example a program will take a different action if an exam mark is a pass than if the mark is a fail.

Programming languages use the If... Then... Else... End If construct to execute one set of instructions if a condition is true and another set of instructions if a condition is false.

EXAMPLE

This conditional statement illustrates an If statement without an Else.

IF Month = 6 THEN SEND ["The month is June."] TO DISPLAY

EXAMPLE

This conditional statement illustrates an If statement with an Else.

IF Speed > 30 THEN

    SEND ["Too fast!. Slow down."] TO DISPLAY

ELSE

    SEND ["Well done. Nice speed."] TO DISPLAY

END IF

ITERATION

Iteration is the process where programs repeat a group of instructions two or more times. Iteration is also known as repetition and looping. Iteration makes programs more efficient by inserting the code to be repeated only once rather than having the same code inserted into the program several times.

FIXED LOOPS

A fixed loop is a when a group of instructions is repeated a set number of times.

EXAMPLE

The following example illustrates the use of a fixed loop to display the squares of whole numbers from 0 to 20. The loop counter (in this case Number) goes from 0 to 20.

FOR Number FROM 0 TO 20 DO

SEND [Number ^ 2] TO DISPLAY

END FOR

EXAMPLE

The following example shows a fixed loop in the games development program Scratch. This loop is repeated exactly 10 times to perform an animation by changing a costume every tenth of a second.

CONDITIONAL LOOPS

A conditional loop is when a group of instructions is repeated until a condition is true.

An example of a conditional loop is a Do... Loop Until. The instructions could be executed only once if the condition is true the first time through the loop or the instructions could be repeated many times until a condition is true.

DON'T FORGET

Input validation is an example of a conditional loop where a loop is used to repeatedly enter an item of data until it is sensible. The data could be valid the first time that it is entered or it could take many repeated attempts before it is accepted by the program.

EXAMPLE

The following example shows a conditional loop in the games development program Scratch. A superhero is given three lives but if he/she touches a baddie then the number of lives is reduced by one. The number of times that the loop is repeated is not fixed, but the loop will continue until the number of lives falls to zero.

THINGS TO DO AND THINK ABOUT

The programming languages that you use for your practical work will have their own means of implementing sequence, selection and iteration. You should think about when sequencing, selection and iteration are required in your own programs.

DESIGN NOTATIONS

STRUCTURE DIAGRAMS

It is much easier for a human being to solve a series of small problems than one large complex problem. A structure diagram is used to split a program up into smaller, more manageable parts. This is performed in a series of steps called stepwise refinement in which a large problem is broken down into parts and then those parts themselves are further broken down into smaller parts. This process is repeated until the parts are small enough to be easy to solve.

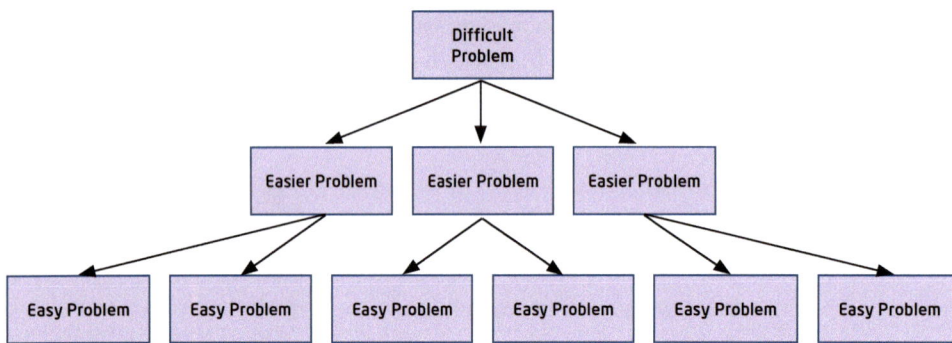

A different symbol is used in a structure diagram to make it clear if sequencing, selection or iteration is taking place.

The different symbols are given below:

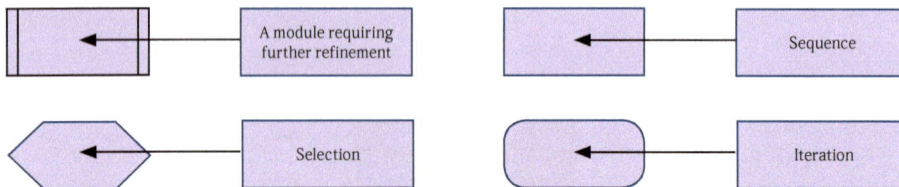

Structure diagrams can be used at the design stage to illustrate the programming constructs of sequence, selection and iteration.

JUST A WEE NOTE

For the assignment component of this course you are required to write a program using a programming language that you have studied in this course. You must design the software as well as creating the program to meet the standards of the assessment.

DON'T FORGET

The approach here is "divide and conquer." It is much easier for a human being to solve several small problems than one large, difficult problem.

SEQUENCE

Sequence is where a list of instructions is carried out one after another.

EXAMPLE

The structure diagram below shows the sequence of steps required for a program which calculates and displays the volume of a cuboid.

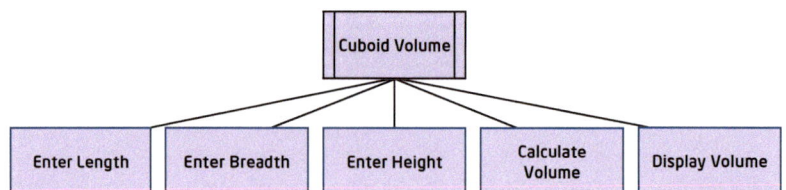

SELECTION

As mentioned previously, selection is where different sets of instructions are carried out depending upon whether a condition is true or false.

EXAMPLE

The structure diagram below shows the steps required for a program which enters the name of a student and an exam mark and gives a message stating if the mark is a pass or a fail.

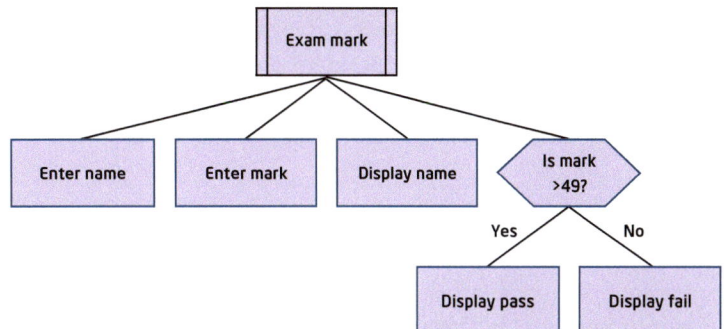

ITERATION

Iteration is where groups of instructions are repeated.

EXAMPLE

The structure diagram below shows the steps required for a program which calculates the number of adults and children in a group of 20 people by entering their ages.

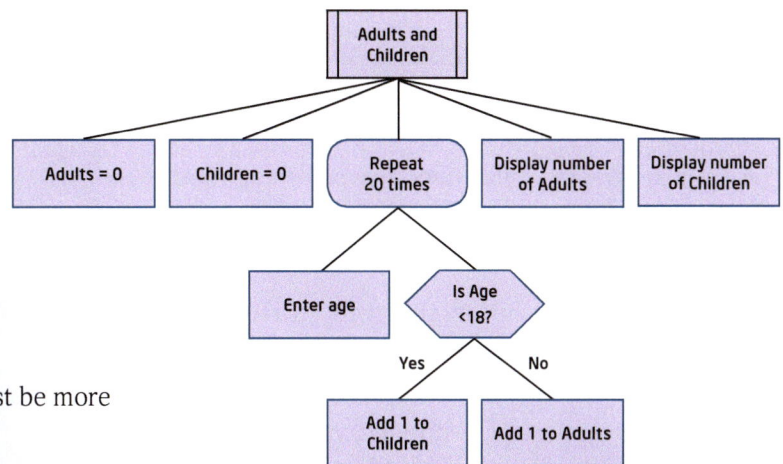

COURSE IDEA

A state in the USA has a law that there must be more adults than children on a minibus.

A program enters the number of men, women, boys and girls on a minibus. The program then calculates the number of adults and children and displays a message stating if the minibus has a legal number of adults and children or not.

Draw a structure diagram to design this program.

Use the correct symbols for sequence, selection and iteration.

A solution is shown on p94.

SUMMARY

Before a program is written, it must be designed using an appropriate design notation. The examples in this spread illustrate how to represent the design of sequence, selection and iteration in a structure diagram.

THINGS TO DO AND THINK ABOUT

Illustrate the design of a program that you have written recently in a structure diagram, indicating sequencing, selection and iteration control constructs.

TESTING AND DOCUMENTING SOLUTIONS

TESTING

Programs are not randomly tested. It is essential to make sure that the program gives correct results when dealing with as wide a variety of possible inputs. A program should be tested methodically with normal data, extreme data and exceptional data.

Normal

One set of test data should be chosen to test that the software gives correct results for everyday data which is within the expected range of values.

For example if a program is entering a percentage mark then normal data could be 72 and 45.

Extreme

One set of test data should be chosen to see if the software can handle data which lies on the boundaries of possible data.

For example if a program is entering a percentage mark then extreme data could be 0 and 100.

Exceptional

One set of test data should be chosen for extreme cases to test if the software can deal with unexpected data without crashing.

For example, if a program is entering a percentage mark then extreme data could be 101, -40, Yes, Eighty, and so on.

EXAMPLE

A program enters the number of goals scored by a footballer in a season. The program then displays a message stating if the footballer is paid a bonus or not. (A bonus is paid to a player who scores more than nine goals.)

The following are examples of normal, extreme and exceptional test data that could be used to test this program. A reason is given for choosing each test data together with the expected results.

Normal test data	17
Reason for choice	This data has been chosen to test for everyday data.
Expected results	Message: "Bonus paid."
Extreme test data	9
Reason for choice	This data has been chosen to test for data that lies on the boundary.
Expected results	Message: "Bonus not paid."
Exceptional test data	Six
Reason for choice	This data has been chosen to test for invalid data.
Expected results	An error message is given and then the number of goals must be re-entered.

DON'T FORGET

Several sets of test data should be created to put a program through its paces and make sure that it will cope with all possible inputs from the user.

COURSE IDEA

You must also make sure that you comprehensively test your own programs in your practical work by supplying normal, extreme and exceptional test data.

Look at the last two programs that you have written.

Write down a set of normal, extreme and exceptional data to test each program. Try out your programs with the sets of test data.

READABILITY OF CODE (INTERNAL COMMENTARY, MEANINGFUL VARIABLE NAMES)

A readable program is a program that is easily understood by another programmer.

Programs are made readable by using techniques that include inserting internal commentary, using meaningful variable names and indentations.

Internal Commentary

Programming languages allow the programmer to insert comments to explain what the instructions are doing. The comments are not executed when the program is executed but are only there to help a programmer make sense of the program code.

Meaningful Variable Names

Variable names are the labels a programmer gives for items of data used by the program. It is important to choose names that relate to the data in a meaningful way. Variable names such as BestScore and WorstScore make it much easier to understand the code than variable names such as B and W.

READABILITY OF PROGRAMS

EXAMPLE

The following program illustrates the readability of programs.

Program 1 is essentially the same program as program as Program 2 but Program 2 is much more readable because it uses internal commentary and meaningful variable names.

The example is given in the Visual Basic programming language.

```
Program 1
Dim P As String
Dim Q As Integer
Dim R As Integer
Let P = InputBox("Enter dog name.")
Let Q = InputBox("Enter dog age.")
If Q < 4 Then
Let R = 7 * Q
Else
Let R = 4 * Q + 9
End If
MsgBox ("Dog's age: " & Q)
MsgBox (P & " would be " & R & " years old if human.")
```

```
Program 2
'Declare variables
Dim DogName As String
Dim DogAge As Integer
Dim HumanAge As Integer
'Enter the dog data from the user
Let DogName = InputBox("Enter dog name.")
Let DogAge = InputBox("Enter dog age.")
'Calculate the age of the dog if it was a human
If DogAge < 4 Then
    Let HumanAge = 7 * DogAge
Else
    Let HumanAge = 4 * DogAge + 9
End If
'Display a suitable the results
MsgBox ("Dog's age: " & DogAge)
MsgBox (DogName & " would be " & HumanAge & " years old if human.")
```

SUMMARY

Programs often need to be re-visited in the future to make changes. Making programs readable by using internal commentary and meaningful variable names makes this process quicker and easier.

THINGS TO DO AND THINK ABOUT

Use a search engine to research how internal commentary is inserted into the programing languages Visual Basic Express, Scratch, Python and JavaScript.

QUESTIONS 1

QUESTION 1

Copy and complete the following sentences by filling in the missing words.

(a) The _____ number system uses only the digits 1 and 0. These are given the name _____ .

(b) A group of _____ bits is called a byte.

(c) A Megabyte is the next unit of storage larger than a _____ .

(d) A _____ is the next unit of storage smaller than a Petabyte.

(e) ASCII codes are used to store _____ on a computer system.

(f) The largest positive number that can be stored in a byte is _____ .

JUST A WEE NOTE

The questions in this spread are based on the topics "Binary Representations" and "Data Types and Structures". Revise these two spreads if you are struggling to answer a question.

QUESTION 2

Convert the following 8 bit binary numbers into decimal.

(a) 00010100 (b) 00001111 (c) 01000010 (d) 01111101

(e) 10000100 (f) 10000011 (g) 10101010 (h) 11111111

QUESTION 3

Convert the following decimal numbers into 8 bit binary.

(a) 13 (b) 21 (c) 97 (d) 131

(e) 127 (f) 160 (g) 200 (h) 255

QUESTION 4

Sophie uses a computer that has a hard disc drive with a capacity of 2 Terabytes.

(a) How many USB memory sticks each with a capacity of 32 Gigabytes would have the same capacity as the hard disc drive?

(b) Sophie has a large number of images stored on her computer's hard drive that she has taken with her digital camera. She wants to copy all of the images on to the 32 Gigabyte memory stick.

How many photos can the USB stick store?

One of the images is shown on the right. (Assume that all of the images have the same filesize.)

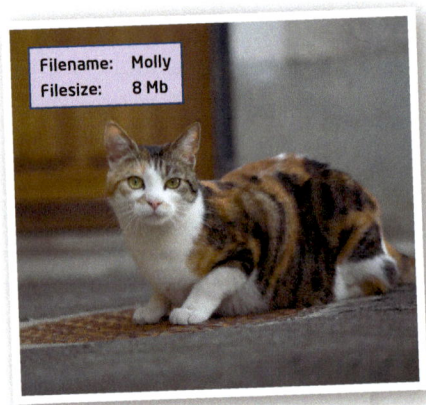

Filename: Molly
Filesize: 8 Mb

QUESTION 5

Shown below is some code from **three** different programming languages.

(a) Which of these programs is written in the computer's own language?

(b) What name is given to program instructions that are written in the computer's own language?

Program 1
```
11101001   1100001000101000
01010011   0000110010111000
00011100   1111001100101001
11001101   0000101011111101
01010101   1100000100001100
11111001   0010101100110011
10101011   0000001000100011
```

Program 2
```
Dim Length As Integer
Dim Breadth As Integer
Dim Height As Integer
Dim Volume As Integer
Length = InputBox("Please enter the length.")
Breadth = InputBox("Please enter the breadth.")
Height = InputBox("Please enter the height.")
Volume = Length * Breadth * Height
MsgBox ("The volume of the cuboid is " & Volume)
```

Program 3
```
when clicked
set points to 0
forever if touching color ?
  change points by 1
  play drum 48 for 0.1 beats
  wait 1 secs
```

(c) (i) What size of space in a computer's memory is needed to hold a single character?

(ii) Including the full stop, how much storage does the following text require?

Somewhere over the rainbow.

QUESTION 6

A program is used for processing a school's sports day tournaments. The program uses numeric variables to store times for the running events and distances for the field events.

Explain why an INTEGER data type would not work for storing these variables.

QUESTION 7

A variable is declared as an Integer data type.

Which of the following items of data can it store?

(a) 3   (b) "Dagger"   (c) -10   (d) 2.5
(e) 64,000   (f) 0   (g) 0.25   (h) 8¾
(i) -273   (j) Seven

QUESTION 8

A computer game simulates a football match between two teams. The game displays the names of the teams and the goals scored by each team.

(a) Which data types would be used to store the team names and the goals scored by each team?

(b) The program also displays other statistics apart from the number of goals for each team.

Suggest **three** other variables that the program might store apart from the team names and goals and state the data type used by each variable.

QUESTION 9

When programs declare variables they specify the data type of the variables.

THINGS TO DO AND THINK ABOUT

Although there is not an external exam for the National 4 course you are still asked to answer written questions on the theory as part of the learning outcomes for the unit assessments.

(a) Copy and complete the Dim statements in the code below by choosing either a STRING or an INTEGER data type.

```
Dim FormClass as ......
Dim Boys as ......
Dim Girls as ......
Dim Total as ......
FormClass = InputBox("Enter name form class.")
Boys = InputBox("Enter number boys.")
Girls = InputBox("Enter number girls.")
Total = Boys + Girls
If Total > 25 Then
        MsgBox ("That's a big class!")
Else
        MsgBox ("That's not too big a class.")
End If
```

(b) Explain why you chose each data type.

QUESTION 10

A quiz App asks a user to enter the name of a sport and then asks ten questions on that sport. The questions have multiple choice answers (A, B, C or D).

The user is then given a score out of ten and a grading (Excellent, Good, Average, Poor, Very poor) on their performance.

Describe how the quiz App uses INTEGER and STRING variables.

QUESTIONS 2

QUESTION 1

1   Re-write both of the following instructions more efficiently by using a different arithmetic operator.

+	-	*	/	^

(a)   The following instruction is used to treble the score of a player in a game.

TrebleScore = Score + Score + Score

(b)   The following instruction is used to find the volume of a cube.

CubeVolume = Length * Length * Length

QUESTION 2

Each of the following instruction contains errors in the use of arithmetic operators. Re-write each instruction with the error corrected.

(a)   Area = Length x Breadth

(b)   Perimeter = 2 * Length + Breadth

(c)   UnitsUsed = PreviousMeterReading - PresentMeterReading

QUESTION 3

In a game a player throws a score with two dice and wins an extra 10 bonus points if a total score of more than 7 is scored. The program code is shown below but there are two errors. Describe the two errors.

Dim Dice1 As Integer
Dim Dice2 As Integer
Dim Total As String
Dice1 = InputBox("Please enter the score for dice 1.")
Dice2 = InputBox("Please enter the score for dice 2.")
Total = Dice1 + Dice2
If Total > 7 Then
        Total = 10
End If

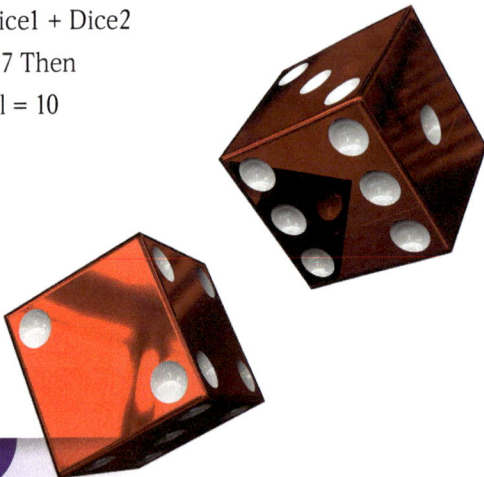

QUESTION 4

Examine the following program code:

Dim Mark As Integer
Dim Total As Integer
Dim Count As Integer
Total = 0
Count = 0
While Count < 5 DO
        Mark = InputBox("Please enter a mark.")
        Total = Total + Mark
        Count = Count + 1
End While
MsgBox (Total / Count)
Explain the purpose of this code.

QUESTION 5

Adults in the United Kingdom are entitled to a bus pass once they reach the age of sixty.

Write a program that will enter the name and age of an adult and display a message stating if the person is entitled to a bus pass or not. The code should start by declaring suitable variables with their data types.

(You can write the code in any language that you choose.)

QUESTION 6

The Scratch program shown below processes numbers stored in the variables Number1, Number2 and Number3.

What is the value of Number1, Number2 and Number3 after this code is executed?

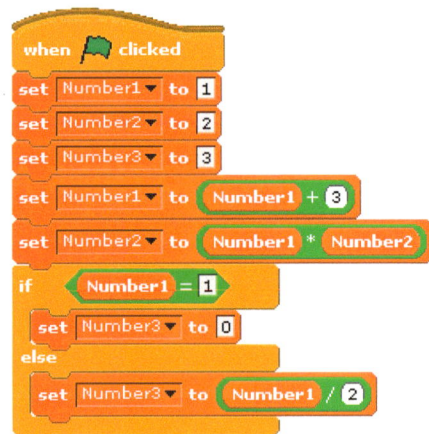

```
when clicked
set Number1 to 1
set Number2 to 2
set Number3 to 3
set Number1 to (Number1 + 3)
set Number2 to (Number1 * Number2)
if (Number1 = 1)
  set Number3 to 0
else
  set Number3 to (Number1 / 2)
```

QUESTION 7

If statements are used in programming to allow the program to take one action if a condition is true and another if a condition is false.

Write down the text that is displayed in the message box for each program.

```
Program A
SET Dice1 TO 5
SET Dice2 TO 2
SET Total TO Dice1 + Dice2
IF Total = 7 THEN
    SEND ["You win."] TO DISPLAY
ELSE
    SEND ["Throw again."] TO DISPLAY
END IF
```

```
Program B
SET Dwarf TO "Dopey"
IF Dwarf = "Sneezy" THEN
    SEND ["Take hanky!"] TO DISPLAY
ELSE
    SEND ["Don't take hanky!"] TO DISPLAY
END IF
```

QUESTION 8

A word processing program uses variables which are STRING and INTEGER data types. The software also has features that use programming constructs to make decisions and to repeat instructions.

(a) Describe two examples of a String data type and two examples of an Integer data types that a word processing program would use to store data.

(b) Describe how a feature of word processing software would use an If... programming construct to make decisions.

(c) Describe how a feature of word processing software would use looping to repeat instructions.

QUESTION 9

Programs use can repeat instructions using fixed and conditional loops.

(a) State if each of the programs shown below is using a fixed loop or a conditional loop.

```
Loop A
RECEIVE Number FROM KEYBOARD
FOR i FROM 1 TO Number DO
    SEND [i ^ 2] TO DISPLAY
END FOR
```

```
Loop B
REPEAT
    RECEIVE PINCode FROM KEYBOARD
    IF PINCode = 1024 THEN
        SEND ["Welcome to your account."] TO DISPLAY
    ELSE
        SEND ["Incorrect PIN! Try again."] TO DISPLAY
    END IF
UNTIL PINCode = 1024
```

(b) Explain the function of each program.

QUESTION 10

A loop and the output that it will produce is shown below.

```
FOR Number FROM 1 TO 5 DO
    SEND [Number * 2] TO DISPLAY
END FOR
```

Output
2
4
6
8
10

Re-write the loop and edit it so that it produces each of the following outputs.

Output A	Output B	Output C	Output D	Output E
3	3	6	1	1
6	6	7	4	8
9	9	8	9	27
12	12	9	16	64
15	15	10	25	125
	18		36	
	21		49	
	24			

JUST A WEE NOTE

The questions in this spread are based on the topics "Expressions and Arithmetic Operators" and "Sequencing, Selection and Repetition". Revise these two spreads if you are struggling to answer a question.

THINGS TO DO AND THINK ABOUT

The written questions in this spread are designed to help you understand the concepts underlying your practical work on programming. Working through these questions will help to develop your programming skills.

SOFTWARE DESIGN AND DEVELOPMENT

QUESTIONS 3

QUESTION 1

Once a program has been completed it is important that it is tested to locate and remove any errors.

Select some of the following words to copy and complete the blanks in the sentences.

new, exceptional, invalid, extreme, correct, normal

(a) To see if the software can handle data on the boundaries of valid data it should be tested with _____ data.

(b) _____ data should be chosen to test that the software can cope with unexpected data without crashing.

(c) _____ data is chosen to test that the software gives correct results for commonplace data which is within the expected range of values.

QUESTION 2

A program enters the number of boys and girls in a registration class.

The program then displays a message saying whether there are more boys, more girls or the same number of pupils in the class.

(a) Give three sets of test data (normal, extreme, exceptional) that could be used to test the program.

(b) Give a reason why you chose each set of test data.

(c) Give the expected output from each set of test data.

QUESTION 3

The program below enters a student's name and percentage exam mark. The program then displays a message stating if the student passed (pass mark 50%) or failed.

Suggest two ways in which the program could be made more readable.

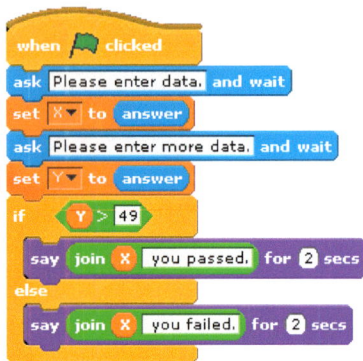

QUESTION 4

A programmer is writing part of a program which enters the number of living grandparents a child has. The number is validated to be in the range 0 to 4.

The programmer tests the code by entering 3 which is accepted by the program. The programmer then concludes that the programming is correct.

(a) Explain why the programmer cannot be sure that the program is correct without further testing.

(b) Supply two other sets of test data that would test the program more fully and give a reason why you chose each set of data.

QUESTION 5

Sam is a programmer and loves eating fruit. When he writes programs he uses the names of fruits for the variables in his programs. Part of the code of one of his programs is shown below.

IF Grapefruit > 30 THEN
    Pomegranate = "Too fast!"
ELSE
    Pomegranate = "Good speed"
END IF

(a) What effect will this have on the readability of the program code?

(b) How can Sam make the code more readable?

QUESTION 6

Name two design notations that a programmer can use to represent the structure of a program.

22

QUESTION 7

A program enters an age of a person and gives a message stating if the person can vote or not.

You need to be 18 to be able to vote.

Copy and complete the structure chart below to show the steps to solve this problem.

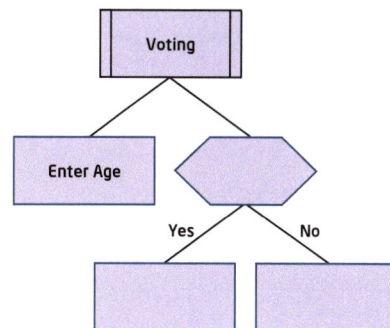

QUESTION 8

A program enters 20 marks and makes a count of the number of pass marks and the number of fail marks.

It then displays the number of passes and the number of fails. (The pass mark is 50)

The structure chart below shows a design of the program structure but it has four errors.

Draw the structure chart with the errors corrected.

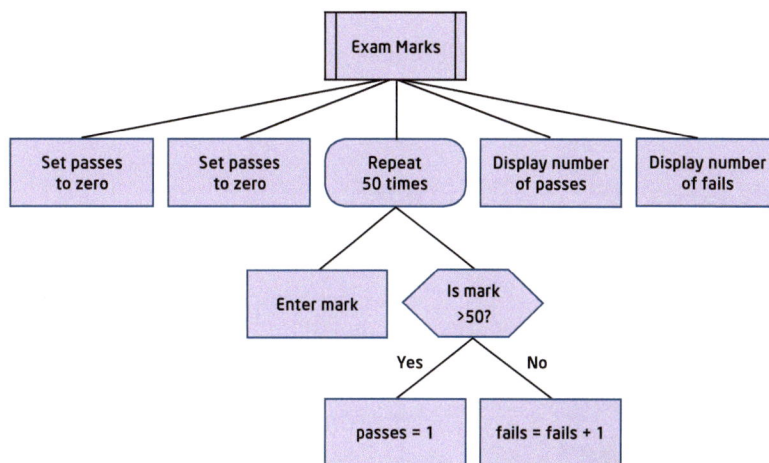

QUESTION 9

A program enters the names and ages of two brothers. It then calculates and displays the name of the oldest brother.

Put together a structure chart to solve this problem using the parts shown below.

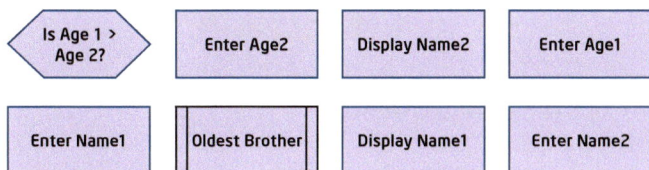

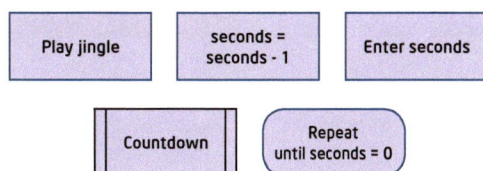

JUST A WEE NOTE

The questions in this spread are based on the topics "Testing and Documenting Solutions" and "Design Notations". Revise these two spreads if you are struggling to answer a question.

QUESTION 10

An app called Countdown enters a number of seconds from the use then counted down to zero at which point a jingle is played.

Put together a structure chart to solve this problem using the parts shown below.

THINGS TO DO AND THINK ABOUT

You are required to design the structure of your programs for the assignment task. Working through the questions in this spread will help you understand the principles of structure charts which can be used for this purpose.

LEARNING OUTCOMES AND UNIT ASSESSMENT

INTRODUCTION

Each of the units Software Design and Development and Information System Design and Development require you to achieve an assessment standard in a set of learning outcomes. Some of these assessments are question based, some involve practical work and others require you to research and report.

In the Software Design and Development unit there are three learning outcomes.

These are listed below.

OUTCOMES

Outcome 1

Explain how simple programs work drawing on understanding of basic concepts in software development.

Outcome 2

Develop short programs using a software development environment.

Outcome 3

Produce a short factual report on a contemporary software-based application.

DETAILS OF THE OUTCOMES

Each of the three learning outcomes has several parts. All of the subsections must be achieved to gain a pass for the outcome.

Outcome 1

This is a written outcome in which you have to show an understanding of how a program works by explaining parts of its code.

There are three subsections to this outcome.

1.1 Reading and explaining code

1.2 Describing the purpose of a range of programming constructs and how they work

1.3 Explaining how data and instructions are stored

The range of programming constructs should include expressions, sequence, selection and iteration.

Outcome 2

This is a practical outcome in which you have to develop short programs to implement a range of programming constructs. You also have to test your solutions with supplied test data and give evidence of test runs.

ONLINE

You can find more information on the unit assessments for National 4 courses on the Scottish Qualifications Authority website, search for 'N4 Computing' at www.sqa.org.uk

DON'T FORGET

Not all schools will assess this outcome in exactly the same way. You might be given a program listing and asked to explain the purpose of parts of the code or asked to explain the effect on the program of changing parts of the code. Some schools might ask for an oral explanation and will not require you to give a written answer. Ask your teacher what you are expected to do to achieve this outcome.

There are four subsections to this outcome.

2.1 Selecting and using expressions, sequence, selection and iteration

2.2 Selecting and using appropriate simple data types, such as numeric (Integer) and String

2.3 Testing digital solutions using supplied test data

2.4 Identifying and rectifying errors in programs

The programs must include at least one construct and at least one data type.

Outcome 3

This is an outcome in which you have to produce a short factual report on a contemporary software-based application.

There are three subsections to this outcome.

3.1 Describing the application

3.2 Explaining how its features relate to programming constructs and data types

3.3 Describing its impact on the environment or society

Your report does not need to be a word processed document. You could use a presentation package or you could produce a small website for the report. Your report is not expected to be a very lengthy and time consuming task. The amount of content would typically equate to about a page or so of text in a word processing document. You are certainly not expected to write a 10 page document.

Your teacher will be able to advice you on the content and length required for your report.

JUST A WEE NOTE

Learning Outcome 3.3 asks you to describe the impact of the application on society OR the environment but not on BOTH the society and environment. Pick the one that suits your chosen application best or cover both points which would be perfectly acceptable for this task.

ONLINE

If you decide to use a presentation for your report, you could think about using the on-line presentation package called Prezi. Prezi is a presentation tool like PowerPoint but it can be used to zoom in and out of elements of the slides and have a more dynamic effect. It can be learned quite quickly and there are on-line tutorials to teach you the basics. Prezi can be found at www.Prezi.com.

SUMMARY

The learning outcomes are a checklist of skills that you have to achieve to pass the unit assessment. The Software Design and Development unit has three Learning Outcomes each of which has several parts.

THINGS TO DO AND THINK ABOUT

You do not have a choice in the form of the assessment tasks for Learning Outcomes 1 and 2. However you do have a choice in Learning Outcome 3 of which application program you use for your report. Make sure that you select an application that is suited to addressing the points you have to cover in your report.

PRACTICE LEARNING OUTCOME 1

INTRODUCTION

To successfully complete Learning Outcome 1 for this unit you must successfully answer a series of question based tasks. Your answers can be completed manually or electronically or assessed by a verbal response to the questions posed by your assessor.

The questions used for this practice learning outcome are presented in the Visual Basic programming language.

There are three sets of questions relating to Outcome 1. To pass this assessment you will have to answer two questions successfully within each set.

JUST A WEE NOTE

It is a common error to be too general in answering this type of question and not to talk about the technical details of code in terms of what the variables and instructions are being used for.

QUESTIONS SET 1: VISUAL BASIC

Read the following program code carefully:

```
Line 1   Dim DogName As String
Line 2   Dim DogAge As Integer
Line 3   Dim HumanAge As Integer
Line 4   DogName = InputBox("Enter dog name.")
Line 5   DogAge = InputBox("Enter dog age.")
Line 6   If DogAge < 4 Then
Line 7       HumanAge = 7 * DogAge
Line 8   Else
Line 9       HumanAge = 4 * DogAge + 9
Line 10  End If
Line 11  ListBox1.Items.Add("Dog's age: " & DogAge)
Line 12  ListBox1.Items.Add(DogName & " is " &
         HumanAge & " in human years.")
```

Q1(a)   Explain what happens when each of these lines of code is run.
Line 1
Line 2
Line 4

Q1(b)   Explain what the If... Else... End If does in Lines 6, 7, 8, 9 and 10.

Q1(c)   Explain how the variable DogAge is stored in the computer.

QUESTIONS SET 2: VISUAL BASIC

Read the following program code carefully:

```
Line 1   Dim SalesPerson As String
Line 2   Dim Mon As Integer
Line 3   Dim Tue As Integer
Line 4   Dim Wed As Integer
Line 5   Dim Thu As Integer
Line 6   Dim Fri As Integer
Line 7   Dim Total As Integer
Line 8   Dim Pay As Integer
Line 9   Pay = 400
Line 10  SalesPerson = InputBox("Enter salesperson name.")
Line 11  Mon = InputBox("How many Monday sales?")
Line 12  Tue = InputBox("How many Tuesday sales?")
Line 13  Wed = InputBox("How many Wednesday sales?")
Line 14  Thu = InputBox("How many Thursday sales?")
Line 15  Fri = InputBox("How many Friday sales?")
Line 16  Total = Mon + Tue + Wed + Thu + Fri
Line 17  MsgBox("The total sales this week was " & Total)
Line 18  If Total > 19 Then
Line 19      Pay = Pay + Total * 5
Line 20  End If
Line 21  MsgBox(SalesPerson & " weekly pay is " & Pay)
```

Q2(a)   Explain what happens when each of these lines of code is run.
Line 1
Line 2
Line 9

Q2(b)   Explain what the If... does in Lines 18, 19 and 20.

Q2(c)   Explain how the Pay variable is stored in the computer.

QUESTIONS SET 3: VISUAL BASIC

Read the following program code carefully:

```
Line 1    Dim Throw1 As Integer
Line 2    Dim Throw2 As Integer
Line 3    Dim Sum As Integer
Line 4    Dim Target As Integer
Line 5    Target = 12
Line 6    Do
Line 7        Throw1 = InputBox("Enter the score on dice 1.")
Line 8        Throw2 = InputBox("Enter the score on dice 2.")
Line 9    Loop Until Throw1 = Throw2
Line 10   Sum = Throw1 + Throw2
Line 11   ListBox1.Items.Add("The total score is " & Sum)
Line 12   If Sum = Target Then
Line 13       ListBox1.Items.Add("Well done you win a fluffy teddy bear.")
Line 14   Else
Line 15       ListBox1.Items.Add("Hard luck you win a plastic duck.")
Line 16   End If
```

Q3(a)   Explain what the Do... Loop Until does in Lines 6, 7, 8 and 9.

Q3(b)   Explain what the variable Target is used for in Line 12.

Q3(c)   What changes would need to be made to this program so that the player wins a large fluffy teddy bear if a score of 10 or more is thrown.

DON'T FORGET

The three question based tasks in this spread are very good practice for Learning Outcome 1 of the Software Design and Development unit. Try these questions and then get your teacher to check your answers and give you advice.

SUMMARY

This assessment requires you to read and explain simple lines of program code that contains Integer and String data types. You must be able to explain what happens when lines of code are run which declare variables, use expressions to assign and return values to variables, perform selection and use iteration with conditional loops.

You must also be able to demonstrate an understanding of how data and instructions are stored in the memory of a computer using binary codes.

THINGS TO DO AND THINK ABOUT

These questions could have been presented in another programming language such as Scratch. Your teacher will use a language that you are familiar with for this learning outcome.

PRACTICE LEARNING OUTCOME 2

INTRODUCTION

Before you are given the unit assessment tasks you will have studied and created programs in your school to develop the necessary skills required to attempt the assessments.

To successfully complete Learning Outcome 2 for this unit you must complete one or more practical programming tasks.

The programs will require you to select STRING and INTEGER data types and use selection, sequencing and iteration programming constructs. You are also required to test your solutions using supplied test data and find and correct any errors in the programming code.

Each solution has to be documented by handing in a printout of the program code and a printout of the test results.

JUST A WEE NOTE

The testing of your solutions for unit assessment is done with supplied data. However for the assignment task which is used for the course assessment you must supply your own carefully chosen test data. This should include normal, extreme and exceptional data.
This topic provides three practice programming tasks that have been produced to allow you to practice for the unit assessments. The tasks are at the same level of difficulty that you can expect for the assessments on this unit.

PROGRAMMING TASK 1

A group of friends is going to the theatre. One of the friends is going to book tickets for the whole group.

Write a program that

- Enters the name of the person making the booking
- Allows the user to enter a number code for one of four types of ticket: 1-Back stalls, 2-Front stalls, 3-Circle or 4-Box
- Enters how many tickets the user wants to buy
- Calculates and displays the name, ticket type, number of tickets and the total cost of the tickets

Ticket	Cost (£)
1-Back stalls	12
2-Front stalls	15
3-Circle	18
4-Box	25

The ticket costs are all a whole number of pounds.

Test your program using these two sets of data:

Test 1		Test 2	
Name	Patricia Davidson	Name	George Mellows
Ticket type	2-Front stalls	Ticket type	4-Box
Number of tickets	13	Number of tickets	5

The output from your program should look similar to the display shown below.

Write the program and then test it with the supplied test data.

```
NAME: Patricia Davidson
TICKET TYPE: 2
NUMBER: 13
TOTAL COST: £195
```

DON'T FORGET

When you do the real unit assessment in your school you must provide documentation of your solution. You must hand in a printout of your program code and also screenshots of the test results.

PROGRAMMING TASK 2

A mobile phone user has a 600 minute limit on calls per month.

Write a program that
- Enters the number of minutes used in each of four weeks

Take one month as 4 weeks for this task
- Calculates and displays the total number of minutes
- Displays a message stating if the user is over the call limit or not

Test your program using these two sets of data: The output from your program should look similar to the display shown below.

Write the program and then test it with the supplied test data.

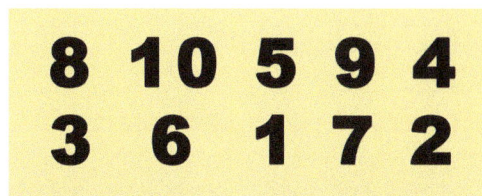

```
Total minutes: 611
You are over the limit this month.
```

Test 1		Test 2	
Week 1	137	Week 1	152
Week 2	159	Week 2	188
Week 3	205	Week 3	91
Week 4	110	Week 4	169

PROGRAMMING TASK 3

A program asks the user to guess a secret number between 1 and 10 until the number is guessed correctly.

Write a program that
- Selects the secret number as 6
- Allows the user to repeatedly enter a guess until the guess is correct

Feedback should be given after each guess stating if the guess is correct or wrong
- Calculates and displays the number of guesses required to guess correctly

Test your program using these two sets of data:

The output from your program should look similar to the display shown below.

Write the program and then test it with the supplied test data.

```
8 10 5 9 4
3 6 1 7 2
```

Test 1		Test 2	
Guess 1	8	Guess 1	6
Guess 2	3		
Guess 3	6		

```
Wrong. Try again!
Wrong. Try again!
Correct. Well done!
Number of guesses: 3
```

SUMMARY

The three programs in this spread are very good practice for Learning Outcome 2 of the Software Design and Development unit. Try these programming tasks and then get your teacher to check your solutions and give you advice.

THINGS TO DO AND THINK ABOUT

Your need to be able to do screenshots of the computer screen to get evidence of your test runs. Screenshots can be done by pressing a key on the keyboard which will be labelled something like "Print Screen". The screenshot can then be pasted into a document by choosing Paste on the Edit menu.

PRACTICE LEARNING OUTCOME 3

INTRODUCTION

To successfully complete Learning outcome 3 for this unit you must complete a report on a contemporary software application. The report requires you to describe the features and the interface of a software package, identify the data types of variables and programming constructs used by the software and describe its impact on the environment and society. The application used for the report does not need to be a large program designed to run on a desktop computer. It could be a mobile app or a program for a video game console.

This is an open book assessment so that you can use the Internet to research an application and gather relevant information but keep a note of the sources as you must include them in your report.

You can ask your teacher for guidance on how to go about this task but remember that your teacher will not give you specific answers and the report must be your own work.

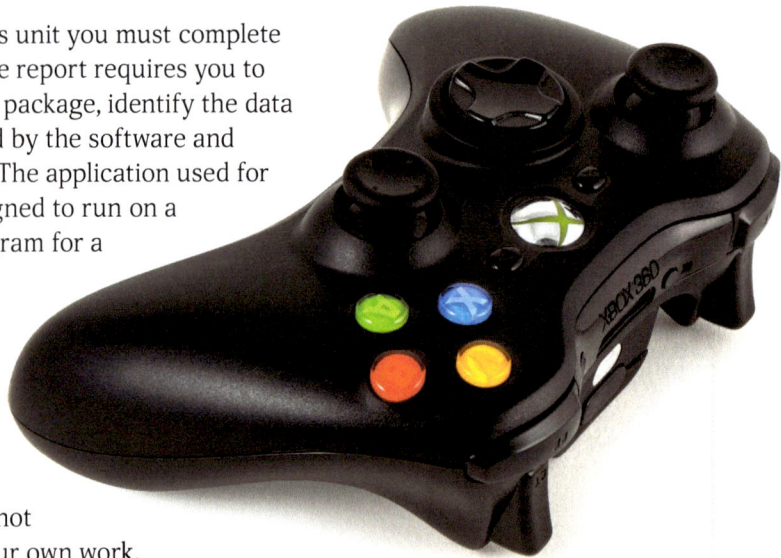

COURSE IDEA

An example report on a software application package called Blender is provided by the SQA. Your teacher can give you a copy of this report but of course it means that you can't use Blender as your choice of package for the unit assessment. Study this report to get an idea of what is expected of you in terms of content and the level of detail.

DON'T FORGET

The evidence you create for this task will be in the form of a report. This does not need to be a word processed document but can be delivered in any appropriate format such as a presentation, a website or a video clip.

PRACTICE TASK

The following task has been produced to allow you to practice for the unit assessments. The task is at the same level of difficulty that you can expect for the assessments on this unit.

This task requires you to research the BBC weather app that is available for mobile phones and tablets and write a report as outlined below.

Step 1

Download the app and install it on your smartphone or tablet computer (it is free!) and explore the features of the app fully. Also use the Internet to investigate its purpose and key features. For example there are YouTube videos giving an overview of this app.

Describe the purpose of the weather app which simply means what it is used for.

Describe its key features by outlining the different features provided by this app.

Describe its interface which means how the user interacts with the software using the touchscreen menus.

Step 2

Describe at least two examples of how the application uses INTEGER and STRING variables.

Describe at least two examples of how the application uses If.End If or repetition programming constructs.

Step 3

Describe the effect the application has on society or the environment.

Describe how this application may affect people's privacy, data security or online crime.

For example you can describe how the application helps to reduce or increase energy use or resources such as paper.

Step 4

Include a page at the end or the report where you state all the sources of your information.

ADVICE

An example of a suitable template for creating your report is provided below.

National 4	Software Development	Learning Outcome 3
NAME		
Step 1 *Name of the application program* *Purpose (What the program is used for)* *Key features* *Interface*		
Step 2 *Use of variables (String and Integer)* *Use of programming constructs (Ifs and Loops)*		
Step 3 *The impact of the chosen application on the environment or society.*		
Step 4 *Sources*		

JUST A WEE NOTE

The application that you report on is chosen by you and not dictated to you by your teacher. You should choose a software-based application that you are familiar with and is suitable as a basis for the report. Before deciding on the application think about whether it is going to let you talk about data types and programming constructs and an effect on society and the environment.

SUMMARY

This section is designed to prepare you for assessment for the Software Design and Development unit. Attempt this task for yourself and then study the solution and explanation given in the next spread. You could also ask your teacher to give you feedback on your report.

THINGS TO DO AND THINK ABOUT

There are several occasions where you will need to produce a report for this course. Make sure that the report is well laid out and clear. Check the spelling and grammar and make sure that the text is easy to read, especially if the report is a presentation.

INFORMATION SYSTEM DESIGN AND DEVELOPMENT

DATABASES

INTRODUCTION

A database is an organised collection of records holding data so that it can be stored and accessed quickly. The advantages of keeping data on a computer include speed of retrieval of information, easier amendments to data, less waste of paper and space and password protection to improve the security of files.

VIDEO LINK

Watch the *GCFLearnFree. org* clip called 'Access 2010: Introduction to Databases' at https://www.youtube.com/watch?v=eXiCza050ug

DATABASE STRUCTURE

File

A database file is an organised collection of records on a particular topic. For example a sports club may keep a file keeping the details on its members or a zoo may keep a file on the details of each of their animals.

Record

A record is the data held on one person or thing. For example a student record in a school database or a stock record in a supermarket stock file.

Field

A field is the term given to one item of data in a record. For example the age field in an employee's record or the price field in a stock record.

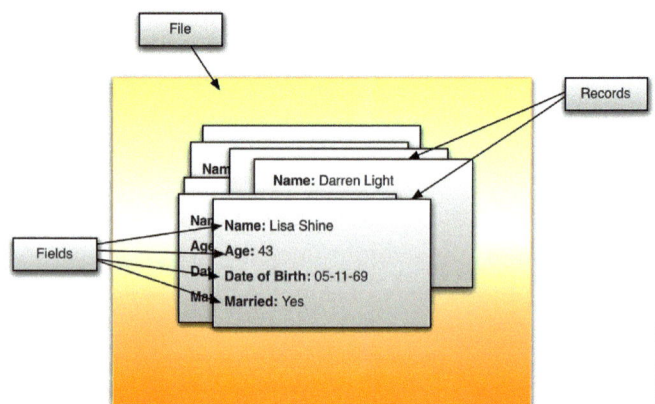

FIELD TYPES

Some fields in a database will contain numbers, other text, some will be storing a date, and so on. Databases allow the field type of each field to be specified so that the data can be stored and processed in a particular way.

Text

A text field stores a string of characters.

Examples of a text field are Surname, Town, Colour, and so on.

Number

A numeric filed stores numbers.

Examples of a numeric field are Age, Height, Population, and so on.

Date

A date field stores a date.

Examples of a date field are Date of Birth, Return to School Date, M.O.T Date, and so on.

Time

A time field stores a time of day.

Examples of a time field are Start Time, Appointment Time, closing time, and so on.

Graphic

A graphics field stores an image.

Examples of a graphic field are Student Photo, Company Logo, Country Flag, and so on.

Calculated

A calculation field (sometimes called a computed field) is calculated from a formula which uses other fields in the record.

For example an Average field could be calculated from three other fields called Test 1, Test 2 and Test 3 using the formula = ([Test 1] + [Test 2] + [Test 3]) / 3

DON'T FORGET

A time field stores a time of day in hours, minutes and seconds and not the time taken for something to take place. For example the time taken for an athlete to run the 100 metres would be stored in a numeric field and not a time field.

DATABASE OPERATIONS

Databases are frequently searched to quickly access records and sorted to arrange records in a certain order such as by date of birth, account number, and so on.

Form Class	Student	Exam	Date of Birth	Hobby
3A	John Edmonds	90	230688	Sky Diving
3A	Harry Simmons	72	100388	Jogging
3A	Sally Green	56	230488	Jogging
3A	Farah Nuggent	33	090188	Chess
3B	Fred Grant	93	290288	Sailing
3B	Peter Morris	67	300588	Reading
3B	Wendy Harrison	45	250388	Football
3C	Gwen Bowie	95	010189	Reading
3C	Alan Smith	76	110588	Sailing
3C	Mandy Barr	65	250389	Jogging
......		......	......	......

Search

A database can be search to select records according to certain rules based on one or more fields. For example, searching a student database for male students who are over 15 years old can be achieved by selecting records where the Sex field = "Male" and the Age field > 15.

Sort

Sorting a database means to arrange the records in ascending or descending order on one or more fields.

Shown below is a student database that has been sorted on the Form Class field in ascending order and then on the Exam field in descending order.

COURSE IDEA

Use a database program to create a database to store the ten records shown in the table above and then select the records for students whose hobby is jogging OR sailing.

Follow these steps:

1 Design the record structure by copying and completing the table shown below. You need to decide a name and a data type for each of the five fields.

Field Name	Field Type

2 Use a database program to create a table to store the data

3 Enter the data for the 10 records shown in the table

4 Create a query to select the records for students whose hobby is jogging or sailing.

(If you are using Microsoft Access select the Create ribbon and then use the Table icon and Query Design icon.)

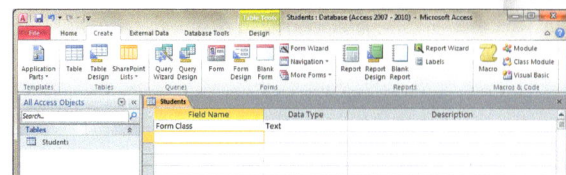

SUMMARY

Database files have an organised structure of records which contain items of data in fields. Different field types exist since fields can store numbers, text, dates, images, and so on. For the practical assessment in this course you need to be able to create a database and select and sort the records.

DON'T FORGET

Ascending order means increasing order. For letters it means in alphabetical order (A, B, C, ...) and for numbers it means getting larger (1, 2, 3, and so on.). Descending order is the other way around. i.e. (Z, Y, X, ...) and (..., 3, 2, 1)

THINGS TO DO AND THINK ABOUT

When creating a database the first step is to design the structure of the records. This involves creating the necessary fields to hold the data and specifying their field types.

The design of the database must be correct or it will have consequences for how the records can be searched and sorted.

WEBSITES

INTRODUCTION

Websites are made up of pages which consist of the multimedia elements text, graphics, video and sound. Other elements such as navigation tabs, tables, hyperlinks, and so on. are commonly used.

Websites can be created using Hypertext Mark-up Language (HTML) and often websites are created using a web page editor. Web page editors allow elements of the website to be dragged and dropped onto the page without the need for writing technically difficult HTML code to achieve the same thing.

BROWSER

A browser is a program that displays web pages and allows the user to navigate around other websites on the Internet. Internet Explorer, Chrome and Firefox are examples of commonly used browsers.

Browsers provide other functions such as:

1   Allowing the user to keep a list of shortcuts to favourite websites so that they can quickly be revisited.
2   Keeping a history of recently visited websites.
3   Accessing webmail to send and receive emails.
4   The settings can be customised to suit the preferences of the user. eg. Controlling which toolbars are displayed, which website is initially displayed, the zoom in/zoom out factor, and so on.

HYPERLINK

A hyperlink is usually a piece of coloured text or an image which, when clicked, provides a connection to another page within the site or to another website. Hyperlinks allow the user to navigate within a site or to find further information in other websites.

DON'T FORGET

An external hyperlink is a link to a different website whereas an internal hyperlink is a link to another page or file within the same website.

URL

Websites can be visited by entering a unique address called a Uniform Resource Locator (URL) into a browser program. The URL is made up of several component parts. These parts include the protocol, the domain name, the path to the file and the name of the file.

For example the URL for a web page about Wimbledon on the BBC website is shown below.

http://www.bbc.co.uk/sports/tennis/wimbledon.htm.

Protocol	Domain name	Pathway	Filename

The protocol is an agreed set of rules between the sender and the receiver that is used to transfer the file. In this case the Hypertext Transfer Protocol (HTTP) is used to transfer a web page.

The domain name is the address of the server computer that is hosting the webpage. Dots are used to separate the different parts (two or more) of the domain name. There is a system for identifying different types of organisation and the country where the site is based.

ONLINE

Go on-line and download some of the websites that are stored in your favourites. Investigate the component parts of the URL displayed at the top of the screen in the browser.

Organisation	Meaning
.com	A company
.edu	An educational institution
.org	A non-profit making institution
.gov	A governmental agency

Country	Meaning
.uk	United Kingdom
.fr	France
.nz	New Zealand
.it	Italy

The pathway specifies the route to the page.

The filename is the name of the actual file that is being accessed.

If the URL is not known for a particular website then the site and other relevant sites can be found by entering suitable keywords into a search engine.

NAVIGATION

Browsers provide several ways to allow the user to move between different websites and web pages. Specific sites can be found by entering the URL into the browser or a search engine can be used to find sites on a certain topic by entering appropriate keywords. Backward and forward arrows can also be used to move back and forth to revisit sites and then move forwards to more recently viewed sites. Websites that are frequently visited can be saved as favourite shortcuts so that they can be accessed quickly without the need for entering the URL.

Most websites also contain a search box to allow the user to go directly to an area of a website that contains the search word or phrase.

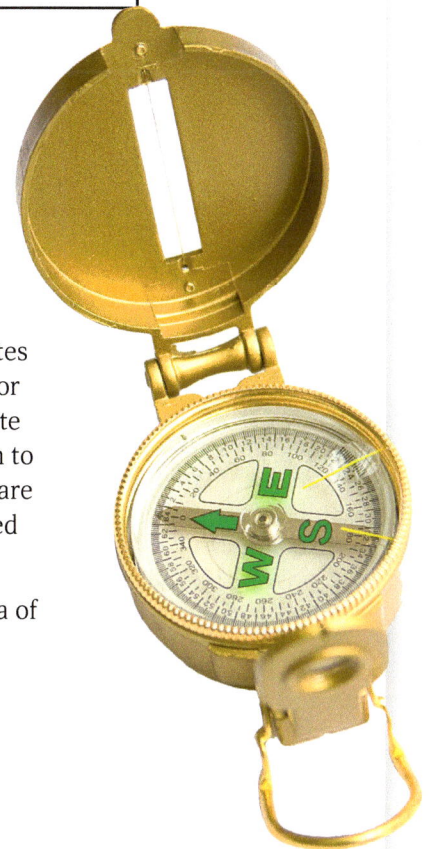

COURSE IDEA

Create a webpage about the Eiffel Tower that contains 3 text articles, at least one image, a video and a hyperlink to another relevant website.

Most schools use Serif WebPlus software which uses the Insert menu to add the elements to the page. If you use another webpage editor explore the menus to insert text, images and so on. and remember to ask your teacher for help if you are stuck.

SUMMARY

Websites are made up of webpages containing text, images, video and sound content. The websites are identified by an address called a Uniform Resource Locator (URL) or can be searched for using a search engine. Links to webpages and other websites are provided using hyperlinks.

THINGS TO DO AND THINK ABOUT

It is important for this course that you can create a simple website with two or more webpages as part of the unit assessment. Make sure that you can insert text, graphics and video into webpages and provide a hyperlink to navigate between the pages.

MEDIA TYPES

INTRODUCTION

Early computer software stored information mainly in the form of text. This was mainly due to the fact that graphics, video and sound data requires a very large amount of storage which was beyond the limits of early computer systems. It is now commonplace for computer programs to store information in a combination of text, graphics, video and sound.

Desktop publishing software uses a combination of text and graphics data and websites use a combination of text, graphics, video and sound data. The different types of data can be imported directly into documents from text, graphics, video and sound files as required.

For example a website about eagles would typically contain textual articles about eagles, images of eagles, videos of eagles in flight and perhaps the birdsong of eagles.

TEXT, GRAPHICS, VIDEO AND SOUND

There are several ways of entering the multimedia elements of text, graphics, video and sound into software.

Text

Text is usually entered with the keyboard but text files can be imported directly into a document from files that have already been created. For example a school magazine could be created by inserting several text files that have already been created by the students into a blank word processing document.

The text can be formatted to change such characteristics as font, fontsize, style, colour, and so on.

Graphics

Graphics can be captured using a scanner or a digital camera and then imported into a document.

This would be essential for photographic images that could not be created by hand but simple drawings such as lines, rectangles, circles, and so on can be created within a document using drawing tools.

Many applications include their own clipart which allows the user to enter keywords to search for suitable images. For example Microsoft Word has clipart built into the program and also has a wider range of images available online on the company's website.

Video

Video can be captured using a digital camcorder or a mobile phone if the quality does not need to be of too high a standard.

Video files are made up of graphics frames that are typically displayed around 20 times per second to create movement and can be extremely high capacity

You can't insert a video or sound into a word processing or desktop publishing document. These applications are designed to create documents with text and graphics such as newspapers and brochures which do not include video and sound.

Audio

Sound can be captured with a microphone and a sound card which converts the data into a form that can be stored on a computer system.

MP3 is a file format for sound that is widely used to store music files on computer and portable devices. Its popularity is due to the fact it uses a method of compression to reduce files to typically about one tenth of their size.

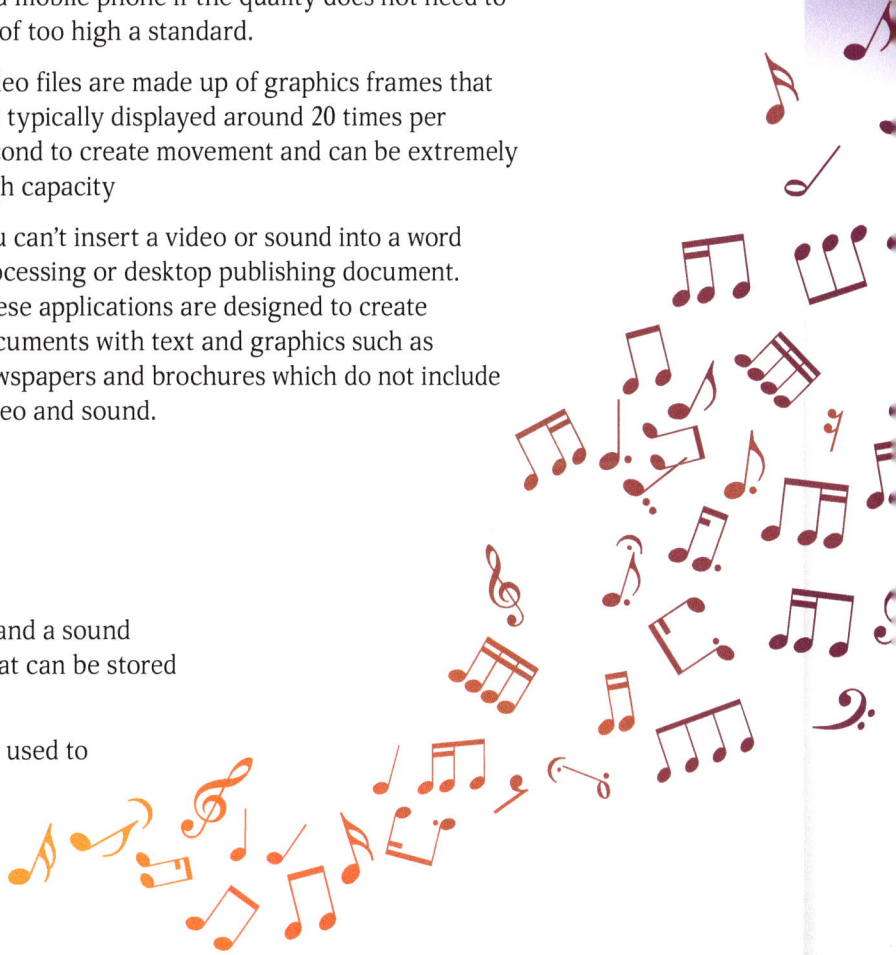

COURSE IDEA

As part of your course and assessment you need to use software to create a simple multimedia website. Most schools use Serif WebPlus software which uses the Insert menu to add text, graphics, video and sound files to the page.

Choose a topic that interests you and then create a folder with one text file, one graphic file, one video file and one sound on that topic.

Then create a blank webpage and use the Insert menu to add these files to the page.

DON'T FORGET

Text, graphics, video and sound can be obtained from other sources such as libraries of materials on CD-ROM, DVD-ROM and downloads from the Internet.

SUMMARY

Many software applications support text, graphics, video and sound. These different media types can be created within the application and/or imported from files that have been created by another application.

THINGS TO DO AND THINK ABOUT

Visit the website www.pcworld.co.uk. Explore its pages and try to find at least one example of each of the multimedia elements of text, graphics, video and sound.

PURPOSE, FEATURES, FUNCTIONALITY AND USERS

PURPOSE

The purpose of an information system basically means what the information system will be used for. The purpose could also be described as what the software has been created for or why it has been made?

The purpose considers what type of user will be accessing the system and what type of device it will run on. For example, the purpose of the system refers to whether the system is for business, leisure or educational use and if it will run on the internet, on a mobile phone or on a desktop computer.

For example, the purpose of YouTube is for all computer users in the world to upload and share videos on smartphones, tablets, laptops and desktop computers.

Another example is a Paris smartphone app whose purpose is to take visitors to Paris on a guided tour of the city's main attractions using video and audio to give a commentary as they go along.

FEATURES AND FUNCTIONS

Describing the purpose of an information system gives an overview of what it is to be used for but a more detailed account requires a description of its features and functions.

Features

The features of an information system is basically what information is being stored. A feature refers to something that an information system has as opposed to the functions, such as sorting and searching, that can be applied to the information.

Functions

The functions of an information system are the ways in which the information is used.

The following are examples of functions of an information system.

- Entering and storing information
- Displaying and formatting the information in different ways
- Searching for particular items of information
- Selecting and sending information to other systems
- Navigating around the different parts of the information system

EXAMPLE

The following example describes the purpose, features and functions of an app that is used for the Edinburgh Festival.

Purpose

The purpose of this app is for Edinburgh Festival visitors to search for, view and purchase tickets for festival events on the go.

Features

The main features of this app are;
- Programme listings of shows and events
- Ticket prices
- Maps of venues
- News of performers and shows

Functions

- Search for shows by name, date, time or type of show (comedy, drama, and so on)
- Locate the nearest shows starting soon
- Check the availability of ticket and prices
- Save shows to favourites and create a personal calendar
- Share shows with friends by email, Twitter or Facebook

TYPE OF USER

The age and ability of the user has to be considered when designing the user interface. If the computer system is for non-technical users then a graphical user interface involving pointing with the mouse is the usual preference. With this type of interface the novice user does not need to remember commands given through the keyboard and can explore pull down menus and icons to make choices. However, an expert user would prefer to use keyboard shortcuts rather than continually switch between moving the mouse and entering data from the keyboard which he/she would find inefficient.

The age-range of the user will also determine the needs of the interface. For example a very young child who can barely read will be able to click on the icons for the tools in a painting program but would find it impossible to perform the same choices through words displayed in menus.

COURSE IDEA

Choose an information system that you use regularly. It could be an app that gives live football scores, an app to download MP3 songs, your school website, and so on.

Describe the information system in a brief report that covers the following points.

Name of the information system: _____

Purpose: _____

Features: _____

Functions: _____

Types of users: _____

SUMMARY

An information system can be described by its purpose, features and functions. For example the purpose of the BBC weather app is to provide a 5 day weather forecast for selected locations in the UK and the rest of the world. The main features of the app are to display temperatures, wind speeds and information on cloud cover, rain, snow, and so on. The functionality includes searching for locations, selecting a specific day for extra weather details, changing the units for temperature and wind speed, and so on.

DON'T FORGET

It is easy to confuse the features and functions of an information system. The features are what information is being stored whereas the functions of an information system are the different ways in which the information is used.

THINGS TO DO AND THINK ABOUT

Learning Outcome 3 for the Information System Design and Development unit requires you to describe the purpose of a contemporary software-based application and its key features and functions. It is difficult to cover every single feature and function but you should give at least three of the main ones. Studying the examples in this section will give you an idea of what is required.

TECHNICAL IMPLEMENTATION (HARDWARE, SOFTWARE, STORAGE, CONNECTIVITY)

HARDWARE

An application program such as Microsoft Word has hardware and software requirements to allow it to be run. There must be enough storage capacity and processor speed as well as an operating system that will provide a platform for the application.

Input and Output Devices

Input devices are used to enter data into a computer system. Commonly used input devices are keyboards, mice, touchpads, scanners, digital cameras, digital camcorders, microphones, and so on.

Output devices are used to display the results of processing in a computer system. Commonly used output devices are monitors, printers, projectors and loudspeakers.

Processor clock speed (Hz)

The clock speed of a processor is measured in Hertz (Hz). Current processors have speeds of several GigaHertz (GHz). The clock speed is a measure of how fast a processor executes a program.

Memory (RAM, ROM)

Main Memory is made up of RAM (Random Access Memory) and ROM (Read Only Memory).

OPERATING SYSTEM

An operating system is a large program that performs basic tasks to manage the hardware and software of a computer system such as inputting data from a keyboard, saving a file to disc, error reporting, and so on.

Microsoft Windows and Apple O.S. are commonly used examples of operating systems.

STORAGE DEVICES

Storage devices are used to permanently store program and data files.

Built-in, External, Portable

Some storage devices are built into the computer case such as an internal hard disc drive whereas others are called external devices because they are outside the computer case and connected to the computer through a USB, FireWire or some other form of connection.

The term portable means that an item of hardware such as a tablet computer can be easily carried around.

RAM is used to temporarily store the users program and data which are currently being executed.

Programs and data can be written to RAM as well as read by the processor.

ROM is used to store programs in a system where the program doesn't changes.

The programs and data in ROM can be read by the processor but ROM cannot be written to.

The contents of RAM can be changed but the contents of ROM cannot be changed.

DON'T FORGET

RAM loses its contents when the computer is switched off but ROM does not.

Magnetic, Optical

Magnetic devices store data by magnetising the surface of a disc or tape.

The capacity of magnetic hard discs range from 100s of Gb to several Terabytes.

Magnetic tape drives have a capacity in the range of 10s of Gb to several 100 Gb.

Optical devices store data on a disc which are written to and read from by a laser.

CD-ROM (Compact Disc Read Only Memory) cannot be written to. The data on the disc can only be read. (700Mb)

CD-RW (Re-writeable) can be read from and written to as often as required.

DVD-ROM and DVD-RW uses similar technology to CDs but have a higher capacity. (4.7Gb)

CONNECTIVITY

Connectivity is a term used to describe the link between computers so that they can communicate and share resources such as printers.

Stand-alone

A stand-alone computer is one which is not connected to any other computers.

Networked

A computer network is two or more computers connected together so that they can share resources and communicate with each other.

LAN/Internet

A LAN (Local Area Network) is a computer network where the computers are in a room, building or cover a fairly small area. The computers are connected

Capacity, Speed

The capacity of a storage device is the amount of data that it can store usually measured in Megabyte, Gigabyte and Terabytes.

The speed of a storage device is how fast it is at reading and writing data from and to the device usually measured in megabits per second.

Read-only, Rewritable

Some storage devices, such as DVD-ROMs, can only be read from and never written to with new data. Other devices, such as CD-RW can be read from and also written to over and over again.

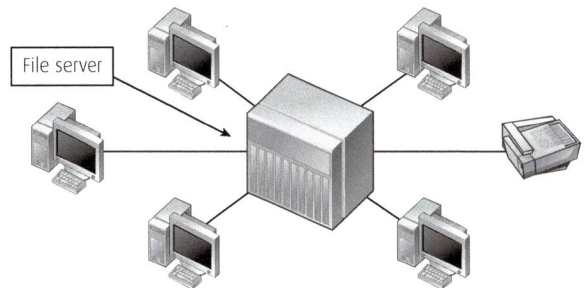

File server

together with cables or sometimes with a wireless connection.

The Internet is a global system of individual computers and computer networks all connected up together.

Wired/Wireless

Wireless connections are slower at transferring data than cable connections but they give more freedom of movement.

Wi-Fi is a wireless connection to the Internet that is used in places such as cafés and airports.

SUMMARY

An application program has system requirements that it needs to run it. These requirements include a minimum processor speed, a minimum amount of RAM, a minimum hard disc capacity and an operating system.

JUST A WEE NOTE

Bluetooth is wireless connection that is used over short distances using radio waves. For example Bluetooth can be used to transfer files between mobile phone or to connect a wireless mouse or keyboard to a computer.

THINGS TO DO AND THINK ABOUT

Investigate the specification of the computer that you use at home. Find out the speed of the processor, amount of RAM, hard disc capacity and the operating system that is installed.

SECURITY RISKS

VIRUSES

A virus is a program that enters a computer (usually without the knowledge of the user) and performs some annoying or harmful action. It is called a virus because it is similar to a medical virus which infects a human being in that it infects the host and spreads to other hosts. A computer virus will damage the healthy operation of the computer and can replicate itself and then spread to other computers. The most common mechanism for viruses spreading is through e-mails. The effect of being infected by a computer virus can vary from a relatively harmless activity such as displaying unwanted messages on the screen to deleting files from memory or even preventing the computer from starting up again.

TROJANS

A Trojan is named after the Trojan horse in Greek mythology which allowed the Greeks to enter the city of Troy by hiding inside a large wooden horse which was presented to the Trojans as a gift. In computing, a Trojan is a piece of software which, when installed on a user's machine, creates a backdoor on a computer that gives malicious users access to the files stored on the computer. Trojans often pretend to be legitimate files presented as gifts in an attempt to persuade users to download them and install them on their computer.

WORMS

A worm is similar to a virus in that it is a program that causes harm to the infected computer. Unlike a virus, the main function of a worm is to replicate itself and also to spread automatically from computer to computer. For example, a worm could send a copy of itself to everyone in an e-mail address book. The worm then replicates and sends itself to everyone listed in each of the receivers' address books. In this way a worm can spread very quickly and cause damage to thousands or even millions of people.

By replicating itself a worm can clog up the memory of a computer and can cause the response of a computer to slow down or grind to a halt. As its name implies, a worm can also tunnel down deeply into folders which can make it very hard to detect and remove.

DON'T FORGET

The word Trojan should always be spelt with a capital "T" and not a small "t" because it refers to the ancient country of "Troy".

HACKING

Hacking is the process of unlawfully breaking into computer systems to gain access to private and confidential information. Some people think that hacking is fun and very clever, but it is a criminal activity and many hackers are put in prison for their crimes. The hacker will often gain access to on-line computer systems from a remote computer which makes him/her hard to catch. The hacker may just look at confidential information and not change the data but can, more seriously, make changes to data such as bank account balances and electricity bills.

Hackers have gained access to computer systems of organisations such as eBay, the US military, international banks and telecommunications companies.

DON'T FORGET

It is important to change your password regularly. Then if it is stolen, it will reduce the time interval in which it can be used to access your private information or to do damage.

COURSE IDEA

A bank uses a website for online banking which allows their customers to view their accounts, transfer money between accounts and pay for goods and services.

Suggest two security risks to the bank's website and describe what precautions the bank can take to guard against the risks.

A solution is shown on page 94.

SUMMARY

Viruses, worms and Trojans are examples of malware which refers to software programs that are designed to do harm or other unwanted actions to a computer system. The word "malware" literally means bad software. Malware, together with hacking, threaten the security of all users of computer systems.

THINGS TO DO AND THINK ABOUT

Computer users need to be protected from threats from viruses, worms and Trojans. Hackers are also a security risk and children need to be protected from access to unwanted material on the Internet. Investigate the security on the computer network in your own school by asking your teacher or network manager what security measures are in place to protect the network.

IMPACT OF IT ON THE ENVIRONMENT AND SOCIETY

ENVIRONMENTAL IMPACT

Carbon Footprint

The emissions of greenhouse gases, in particular carbon dioxide, have a serious contribution to global warming and climate change.

Carbon footprint is a measure of how much carbon dioxide is produced in the making or use of devices such as televisions, cars, aircraft and computing equipment.

The manufacture of IT equipment contributes to the carbon footprint. The making of a single desktop computer requires the burning of 10 times its own weight in fossil fuel.

Using computing equipment uses electricity which is largely produced in power stations by burning fossil fuels such as coal and oil. The waste product of this process is the creation of large amounts of carbon dioxide.

On the other hand, in some respects the use of IT can help to reduce the carbon footprint. For example, the increasing number of people working from home decreases the need for travel. Cars, buses and trains all burn a large amount of fossil fuels.

Another example is that of video conferencing, where meetings take place in a virtual conference using online computers and multimedia hardware devices. Traditional meeting in hotels and conference centres can require the need for air travel which has a large carbon footprint.

Disposal of IT Equipment

Computing technology is constantly improving which means that a state of the art computer bought today will be out of date in a few years' time. Therefore computers, mobile phones, peripheral devices, and so on are frequently disposed of in order to make way for the newer models. The problem then arises of how to dispose of these unwanted items. Computers are made up of plastic, glass and steel and chemicals such as mercury, lead and cadmium. If these computers are randomly thrown away then there are serious consequences for pollution of the environment and contamination of the water we drink and the air we breathe.

Paperless Office

The term "the paperless office" comes from the fact that storing data on backing store devices has a huge impact on the need for paper documents and has an enormous saving on the amount of trees that are needed to manufacture paper.

> **VIDEO LINK**
>
> Watch the video on 'How to recycle computers' at http://www.youtube.com/watch?v=s1cpo_0vbh0 One partial solution is to recycle many of the materials used in computers which can help to save resources and protect the environment.

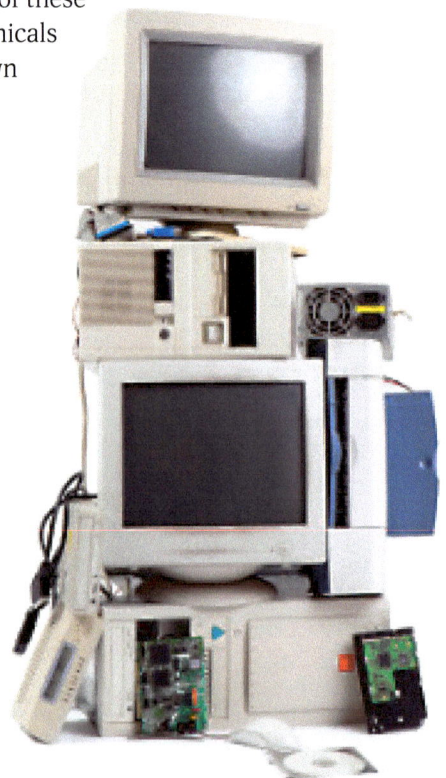

> **COURSE IDEA**
>
> Consider the impact on the environment of the word processing software that is used in your own school. You should focus on the positive and negative effects of the use of this software.
>
> Your report should be approximately 200 words.

IMPACT ON SOCIETY

Some areas in which Information Technology is impacting on society include communication, education, work and entertainment.

Communication

Social media sites have transformed the way that people communicate. Facebook and Twitter are very immediate and widespread means of communication compared to traditional methods such as posting letters.

Education

The way people learn now is very different from the days when all lessons were delivered by a teacher talking at a blackboard/whiteboard. Increasingly teaching is delivered with multimedia content with the students using computing devices to access content on the Internet. Students can also present their work in a more attractive word processed form or through multimedia presentation packages and websites.

Work

More and more people are using computer technology to work from home.

Advantages	Disadvantages
At home you can work the hours that suit you.	There is not the equipment and resources available at home that there is in the office.
There is not the stress of the office environment.	There is sometimes less chance of promotion because you are not part of the office environment.
There is not the time and expense of travelling to work.	People can become socially isolated and miss the company of friends at work.

Entertainment

Up until the second half of the last century the main form of technological entertainment in the home was through a small number of television channels on a small screen and the radio. This has been considerably advanced with the ability to record programs and play DVD and Blu-ray discs. The quality of screens has considerably improved with a considerable increase in size, resolution and now 3D television is becoming commonplace. Gaming is constantly improving the complexity of the games and the quality of the graphics and virtual reality looks like it will be the next major advance.

SUMMARY

IT has an impact on our lives and the planet we live on. It is affecting the way we work and learn and many other aspects of how we go about our lives. It also has both a positive and negative impact on the earth's resources and people's health.

THINGS TO DO AND THINK ABOUT

Health and safety is a major issue in the use of technology. Use the Internet to research how the use of computing equipment can damage our health and the steps that can be taken to guard against these issues.

DON'T FORGET

Apart from carbon dioxide there are other gases that contribute towards climate change. Nitrogen trifluoride NF_3 is produced as a waste product by factories that make flat screen displays. This gas is worse at warming the atmosphere than carbon dioxide but is produced in much smaller amounts.

QUESTIONS 1

QUESTION 1

Mr Strictly works as a maths teacher in Hapsworth High School. He keeps his student exam marks as a percentage in a database. The records in his database are shown below

(a)   How many fields are there in this database?

(b)   Which of these fields should be a numeric field type?

(c)   How many records are there in this database?

QUESTION 2

The record shown below is from a database kept by a small zoo.

State a suitable field type for each field.

QUESTION 3

A stock database in a supermarket contains 544 records. If each record requires 96 bytes of storage what is size of the database file in Kilobytes?

Animal Record

Species	Lion
Date of birth	12/06/2010
Nutrition	Meat
Weight (Kg)	128
Photo	

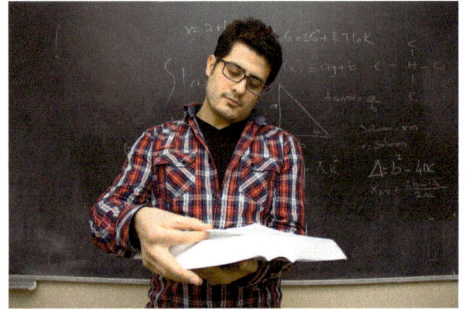

Student	Sex	Form class	Maths
Mandy Metcalf	F	4C	50
Zack Greer	M	4A	87
Walter Winters	M	4C	78
Lilly Porter	F	4D	36
Sophie King	F	4D	67
Andrew Green	M	4B	35
Dianna Davidson	F	4C	51
Ronald Aston	M	4A	68
Heather Carson	F	4C	83
Tom Paterson	M	4A	40
Susan King	F	4B	67
Harold Higgins	M	4A	78
Toni Mcnicol	M	4A	94
Katherine Sainty	F	4B	38
Daphne Dickenson	F	4C	82
John Matheson	M	4D	66

QUESTION 4

A sports shop owner keeps records of 1,280 stock items in a computer database.

An example of a record is shown below.

(a)   State which field in the record should be a calculated field.

(b)   Explain why it is more efficient to make this field a calculation field rather than a numeric field.

(c)   Suggest another field that could be included in the records of this database and give the field type of the field.

QUESTION 5

A sort has been performed on the golf scores database shown below.

Golfer	Nationality	Score	Status
Sam Green	British	67	Professional
Tom Wadkins	U.S.A.	69	Professional
Harry Hook	U.S.A.	70	Professional
Charlie Chippings	British	70	Professional
Sergio Lyle	Spanish	72	Amateur
Luke West	British	73	Professional
David Bush	Australian	73	Professional
Reginald Woods	Canadian	74	Professional
Jack Palmolive	U.S.A.	77	Professional
Nick Major	U.S.A.	78	Amateur

Describe how the database records have been sorted.

Item	Ice Skates
Supplier	Ice World
Quantity	15
Price (£)	24.90
Stock value (£)	373.50

QUESTION 6

A company called Party Fun sells and hires fancy dress costumes, masks and tricks on their website. The URL for a web page displaying celebrity masks is shown below.

http://www.partyfun.co.uk/masks/celebrities.htm

(a) What does URL stand for?

(b) What is a URL used for?

QUESTION 7

Heather has created a website for her school swimming team that includes text about swimming competitions and images of the swimming teams. Apart from text and graphics, suggest two other types of data that Heather could include in her website to make it more appealing to visitors.

QUESTION 8

Most websites have links from the home page to other pages within the site and to other websites.

(a) What is the name of the feature that websites use to provide links?

(b) How does the visitor to a website know what to click on in order to activate a link?

QUESTION 9

The following sentences describe features of websites.

Select some of the following words to copy and complete the blanks in the sentences.

bookmarks, sound, images, hyperlinks, URL, browser, doormats, webpages

(a) Most websites contain text, graphics, video and _____ data.

(b) _____ are used to provide links to other websites.

(c) A _____ is used to specify the address of a website on the Internet.

(d) A _____ is a program that is used to display webpages and to navigate around the Internet.

(e) Most websites have a home page which links to other _____.

(f) Commonly visited websites can be saved as _____.

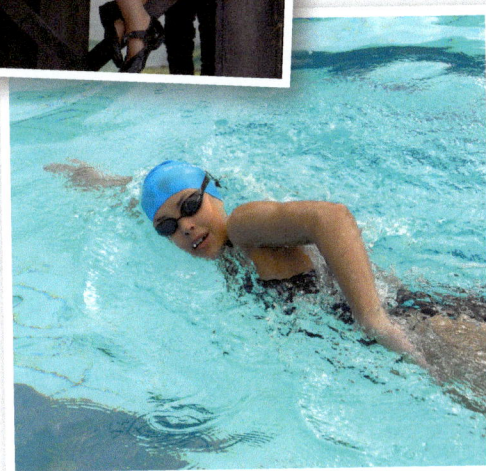

QUESTION 10

Sophie is doing a history project about the Second World War. She went on the Internet and found an excellent site that she could use for pictures and sources for her project. Unfortunately, the next day she could not find the website again using a search engine and couldn't remember the website address.

(a) Apart from using a search engine, how could Sophie find the website again?

(b) What should Sophie do in the future to prevent this sort of problem happening again?

SUMMARY

The questions in this spread are based on the topics "Databases" and "Websites". Revise these two spreads if you are struggling to answer a question.

THINGS TO DO AND THINK ABOUT

Read this book regularly as a study guide but when doing a specific assessment read over the topic that gives help or practice on that particular task.

QUESTIONS 2

QUESTION 1

Select some of the following terms to copy and complete the blanks in the sentences below.

digital camera, sound, text, video, CD-ROM, microphone, graphics, scanner

(a) Multimedia is a computer system that uses the data types of _____, graphics, _____ and sound.

(b) Graphics can be captured with a _____ or a _____.

(c) Desk top publishing is a type of software that is used to produce documents which contain text and _____ but not video and _____.

QUESTION 2

1 Unscramble the following anagrams of terms used in multimedia.

(a) EVOID   (c) MORECHOPIN   (e) IGAME

(b) CARTLIP   (d) SICUM

QUESTION 3

A hockey team want to capture some video clips of the team in action to put on the school website.

(a) Name two hardware devices that can be used to capture video to be entered into a computer system.

(b) State which of the two devices is best suited to capturing the images of the hockey team and justify your answer.

QUESTION 4

State if each of the following is a feature or a function of an information system.

(a) Searching for a player in an app that gives live golf scores in the British Open.

(b) Adding records for new pupils in a school database.

(c) A list of endangered birds in a wildlife website.

(d) Sharing videos on the YouTube website with friends.

(e) Cinemas and times of films on a cinema booking app.

QUESTION 5

Give a brief description of the purpose of each of the following items of software.

(a) A word processing program

(b) The Twitter website

(c) A calendar app on a mobile phone.

QUESTION 6

The age and ability of the user has to be considered when designing the user interface for a software application.

Describe two ways in which the interface can be made suitable for a 5 year old user.

QUESTION 7

Desktop and laptop computers have a backing store device as well as main memory.

(a) Why do computers require a backing store device when they have main memory to store program and data files while they are being executed?

(b) Desktop computers usually have a hard disc drive as their main backing store device while laptops have a solid state drive.

Give an advantage and a disadvantage of a laptop computer using a solid state drive instead of a hard disc drive.

(c) Name a device that can be used to keep backup copies of the data stored on a computer and give two reasons why it is a suitable device.

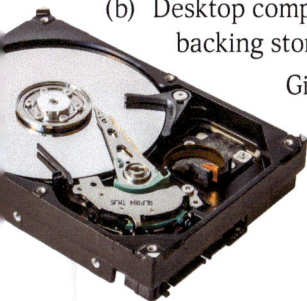

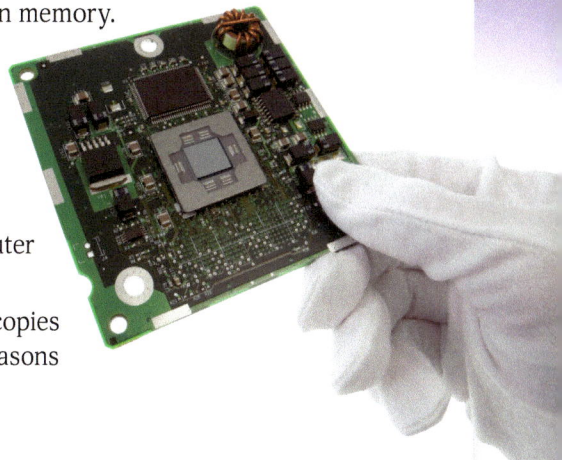

QUESTION 8

Desktop, laptop and tablet are three types of computer.

Given below is a brief description of the computing needs of three people doing different jobs. For each person state which type of computer is most suitable and give a reason for your answer.

A Wendy is an author of children's books. She likes to do her writing outside in the park or in cafés on rainy days.

B Alex is a cricket fan and likes to check the score of cricket matches on the go.

C Ben is a graphic designer who uses a computer to create large posters for international films.

QUESTION 9

Castoffs is a small casting agency company that acts as an agent for actors in the London theatre. They have a small office with six stand-alone computers.

(a) Explain the term stand-alone computer.

(b) Castoff has decided to install a computer network.

Describe two advantages to the company of networking the computers.

(c) The company has to decide if they want to have wires connecting the computers or to go for a wireless connection.

Describe one advantage and one disadvantage of using wires instead of a wireless connection.

QUESTION 10

Select some of the following terms to copy and complete the blanks in the sentences below.

magnetic, CD-ROM, clock speed, read-only, portable, capacity, DVD, operating system

(a) An item or hardware is described as _____ if it is easy to carry around.

(b) _____ and _____ are examples of optical storage devices.

(c) The _____ is a large program that manages the hardware and software of a computer.

(d) _____ is a measure of the power of a processor.

(e) The amount of data that a storage device can hold is called its _____.

SUMMARY

The questions in this spread are based on the topics "Media Types", "Purpose, Features, Functionality and Users" and "Technical Implementation (Hardware, Software, Storage, Connectivity)". Revise these three spreads if you are struggling to answer a question.

THINGS TO DO AND THINK ABOUT

The assessment tasks for this course include question based tasks as well as practical tasks. Study the questions in this spread and ask your teacher for extra examples to get practise on answering questions.

QUESTIONS 3

QUESTION 1

Polly works for a fashion company as a graphics designer.

(a) The computer that Polly uses at work got infected by a virus despite her company having anti-virus software installed.

How could Polly's computer still get infected despite the anti-virus software.

(d) Explain the difference between a virus and a worm.

QUESTION 2

Find three terms in the wordsearch below which are security risks to a computer system.

QUESTION 3

Select some of the following words to copy and complete the blanks in the sentences below.

worm, keylogger, Trojan, hacking, virus, firewall

W	T	Q	H	C	R	B	S	A	I	K
A	R	L	Z	I	Z	E	S	L	C	J
Q	E	S	W	O	R	M	F	D	F	U
S	Y	D	B	Q	F	G	Y	N	H	W
V	H	Y	C	T	E	S	H	A	Z	Q
B	J	E	D	F	U	X	M	J	G	A
G	I	T	I	R	H	D	N	O	B	B
T	V	F	I	J	B	G	A	R	K	F
H	W	V	I	W	S	E	N	T	R	E
Y	T	B	H	D	P	T	M	U	V	T
E	T	W	N	Y	J	L	I	K	D	S

(a) A _____ is a program that enters a computer and performs some harmful action.

(b) _____ is the process of unlawfully gaining access to private and confidential data.

(c) A _____ is a program that appears to be a gift in order to persuade users to download the program onto their computer where it performs a harmful action.

(d) A _____ is a harmful program that clogs up computer systems by replicating itself and burying deep down into folders where it is hard to remove.

QUESTION 4

Henry has bought a new computer to buy goods and services over the Internet.

After a month his computer will not start up giving an error message stating "Critical system files are missing."

(a) What is likely to have happened to Henry's computer?

(b) What precaution could Henry have taken to have protected his computer?

QUESTION 5

A Trojan is a certain type of harmful software that is named after an event in Greek mythology.

Explain why a Trojan is given its name.

QUESTION 6

Thousands of tons of computing equipment are discarded in the UK every year and the amount is increasing.

Why is it that IT hardware is thrown away more frequently than other types of hardware such as kettles and frying pans?

QUESTION 7

The growth of IT equipment has had consequences for the environment.

(a) Explain how using computers contributes to the carbon footprint.

(b) Describe two other ways in which computing equipment can contribute to the carbon footprint apart from their use.

(c) Apart from the carbon footprint, describe another way in which the growth of computing has a damaging effect on the environment.

QUESTION 8

More and more people are working from home than used to years ago because of computing technology.

(a) Suggest two reasons why someone might prefer to work from home.

(b) Describe one way in which working from home is good for the environment.

QUESTION 9

Word processing software has been one of the most successful application programs used in computing technology.

Apart from using up electricity, describe two ways in which using word processing software uses up other resources.

QUESTION 10

Tom works on his computer for long hours in his kitchen. He works at the kitchen table and sits on a breakfast stool but recently has begun to complain about his health.

(a) Describe how Tom's work routine could have a bad effect on his health.

(b) What changes can Tom make to guard against his computer use having a damaging effect on his health?

SUMMARY

The questions in this spread are based on the topics " Security Risks" and "Impact of IT on the Environment and Society". Revise these two spreads if you are struggling to answer a question.

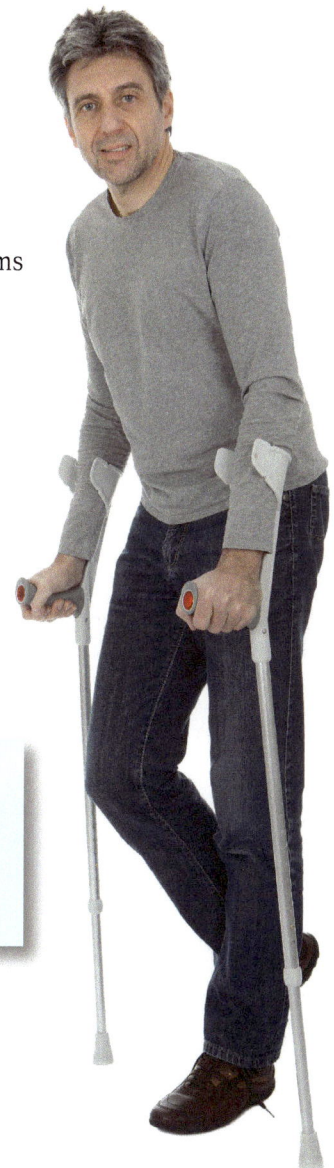

THINGS TO DO AND THINK ABOUT

Visit the website www.pcworld.co.uk and enter the word "security" into the site search box. You will get a list of products that help to maintain the security of computer systems. Apart from anti-virus software, investigate the other types of security that these products have to offer.

LEARNING OUTCOMES AND UNIT ASSESSMENT

INTRODUCTION

Each of the units Software Design and Development and Information System Design and Development require you to achieve an assessment standard in a set of learning outcomes. Some of these assessments are question based, some involve practical work and others require you to research and report.

In the Information System Design and Development unit there are two learning outcomes.

These are listed below.

OUTCOMES

Outcome 1

Develop simple information systems using appropriate development tools.

Outcome 2

Consider a number of factors involved in the design and implementation of an information system by describing it in simple terms.

DETAILS OF THE OUTCOMES

Each of the two learning outcomes has several parts. All of the subsections must be achieved to gain a pass for the outcome.

Outcome 1

This is a practical outcome in which you have to achieve each of the following criteria though the development of one or more information system.

There are three subsections to this outcome.

1.1 Creating a structure and links

1.2 Integrating different media types

1.3 Identifying and rectifying errors

You have to create the structure for an information system and then provide links to connect the parts together.

For example you might create a website with a home page and two other webpages. Hyperlinks would then be used to link the pages together and allow the user to navigate around the website.

The information system must use a combination of text, graphics, video and sound media types. The different types of media can be stored in text, graphics, video and sound files which can then be imported directly into databases, presentations and websites.

You are expected to identify and remove any errors from the software. It is easy not to spot errors in something that you wrote yourself. It is a good idea to get another student to test out your information system who might discover problems that you would know how to avoid.

JUST A WEE NOTE

There are only two Learning Outcomes in the Information System Design and Development unit as opposed to three in the Software Design and Development unit. To pass the National 4 course you must achieve all of the unit assessments in both units and also pass a course assignment task that is based on both units. The course assignment task is covered later on in this book.

ONLINE

You can find more information on the unit assessments for National 4 courses on the Scottish Qualifications Authority website (www.sqa. org.uk).

DON'T FORGET

The criteria for Learning Outcome 1 are designed to cover different types of information system. It does not matter if you use a database, website, multimedia presentation or a mixture of these to achieve these outcomes.

Outcome 2

This is an outcome in which you have to consider each of the following factors in respect of an information system.

There are three subsections to this outcome.

2.1 Its basic features and functionality

2.2 Its hardware, software, storage and connectivity requirements

2.3 The security risks involved in digital communication

The features and functions are the objects provided by the software and the operations that can be performed on the objects. For example, in an information system created using presentation software, the information system has text and graphic objects that can be formatted and animated.

The main issues to consider for the hardware and software requirements are the type and speed of the processor, the amount of RAM, the hard disc capacity and the operating system that the information system will run on.

Connectivity refers to any connection that is required to other computers over a network and the Internet.

Security risks will include a discussion of how vulnerable the information system is to hacking and virus attacks. You must also mention the steps that can be taken to guard against these risks, such as anti-virus software and passwords.

You can find more information on these issues in the "Security Risks" spread in this book.

SUMMARY

The learning outcomes are a checklist of skills that you have to achieve to pass the unit assessment. The Information System Design and Development unit has two Learning Outcomes, each of which has several parts.

THINGS TO DO AND THINK ABOUT

You must achieve the learning outcomes for the unit assessments by yourself. However you should take opportunities to seek advice from your teacher on how to proceed with the assessment tasks. Never expect the teacher to complete a task for you, but you can certainly ask for guidance and feedback on your progress.

PRACTICE LEARNING OUTCOME 1

INTRODUCTION

To successfully complete Learning Outcome 1 for this unit you have to successfully create the structure of an information system which must include links. The information system must also include two or more different media types (text, graphics, video and sound). You are also required to test out the information system and to identify and correct any errors.

JUST A WEE NOTE

Don't worry if your webpages do not follow exactly the design shown above but you should make sure that each webpage has a title, text article, image and navigation bar. The precise positioning of the elements of the page will depend upon your size and shape of graphics, amounts of text and font size, and so on.

ASSESSMENT TASK

You have probably been on lots of holidays that you have really enjoyed. You are going to create a website to present what you consider to be your ideal holiday.

The website will consist of four web pages that will present important features of the holiday. You need to create a Home page and three other web pages.

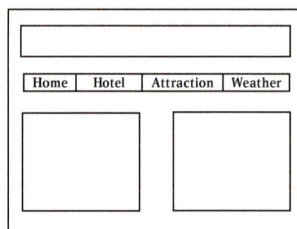

An outline of the contents of each webpage is given below:

- A Home page with a map of where the holiday destination is
- A webpage giving information about the hotel that you are staying in
- A webpage giving information about an attraction that you would visit
- A webpage giving information about the typical weather for the holiday destination

The design of the four web pages you have to create is shown below.

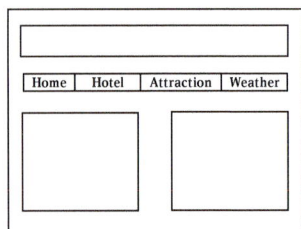

| Home | Hotel | Attraction | Weather |

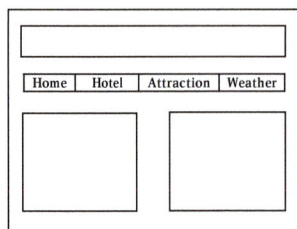

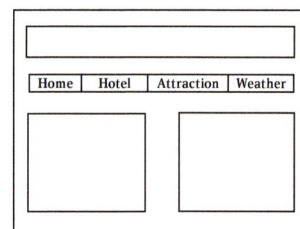

Home webpage   Hotel webpage   Attraction webpage   Weather webpage

Step 1

State your ideal holiday destination and name the software that you will use to create the webpages.

Step 2

Create four graphics files that you will use for the images on the four webpages.

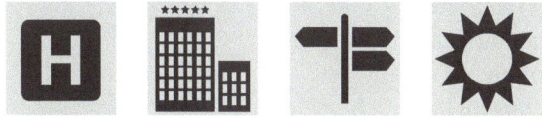

Step 3

Create the web pages as close as possible to the designs shown above.

The titles of each webpage should be at the top of each page and stand out. Use a larger font size/colour/bold, and so on.

Include a description of the fonts, font sizes, font styles, colours, and so on that you used in the website.

Step 4

Place a navigation bar in each of the four webpages or other means to provide the following links between the webpages.

- The website opens with the Home page being displayed.
- In all of the four pages, clicking on the appropriate webpage in the navigation bar will take the user to the desired webpage.

When the map image on the Home page is clicked it will take the user to another website providing information about the holiday destination.

Step 5

Describe any problems or errors you encountered during the creation of your website and give an explanation of how you solved them.

JUST A WEE NOTE

This task is described in terms of using text and images as the two media types to be included in the information system. There is no reason why you can't use video and sound as well but it is certainly important to use text articles to give information about the holiday destination to visitors of the website. Most webpage editors have an Insert pull down menu from which you can select text, image, video and sound.

SUMMARY

This assessment is essentially a practical task in which you create an information system with links and insert different types of media such as text and graphics. It also requires you to write up your solution with screenshots and to describe any errors that you came across and explain how you fixed them. It is probably best to word process your write up but you could use other means to present your solution, for example a presentation package.

THINGS TO DO AND THINK ABOUT

This task involves producing evidence of the completed software solution. Evidence can be gathered from screenshots or by getting your teacher to view your website on screen.

Evidence that the links have been successfully implemented is best done by asking your teacher to check that the links operate correctly. Test your software yourself to make sure that the media types display properly and that the links operate correctly before you ask your teacher to check your solution.

PRACTICE LEARNING OUTCOME 2

INTRODUCTION

To successfully complete Learning Outcome 2 for this unit you must successfully describe the basic factors involved in the design and implementation of an information system. There are three main factors. These include a description of the information system, a description of the hardware and software required to run the information system and a description of the security risks to the information system. To pass this assessment you will have to describe all of the factors successfully.

JUST A WEE NOTE

This assessment requires you to think of examples of security risks to the website. There are a wide variety of security risks but for this task you should concentrate on attacks from harmful software and hackers.

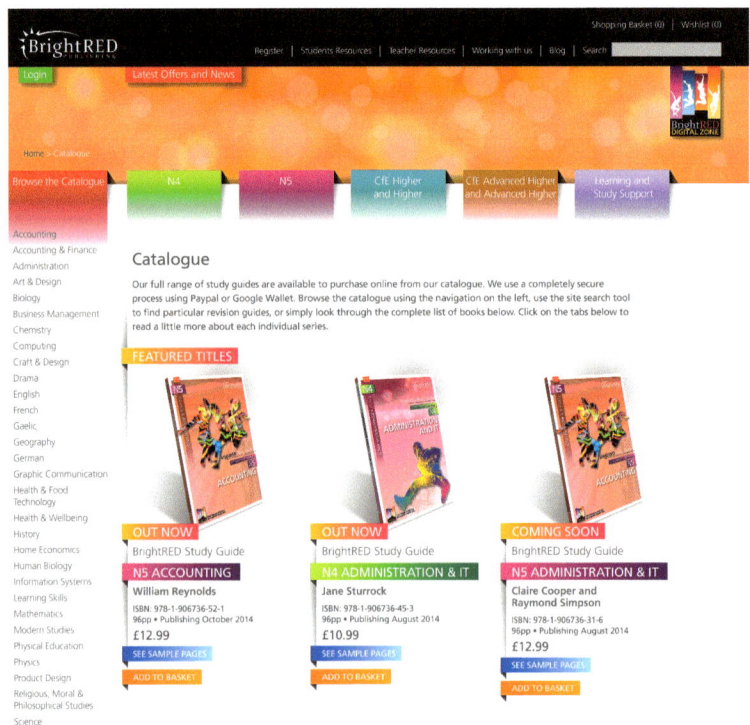

The information system could be a database, website, presentation package, and so on. In this particular practice task you are required to report on a website but your own school could use another type of information system for this assessment. No matter what type of information system your school uses for this assessment the same factors will need to be described in the report.

ASSESSMENT TASK: INTERNET SHOPPING

There are hundreds of thousands of websites that are used throughout the world for the buying and selling of goods and services on-line. You are going to select a site that is used for Internet shopping and produce a report following the steps that are outlined below.

The website must be used for one of the following:

- buying clothes
- buying sports equipment
- buying tickets for events
- buying holidays
- buying mobile phones

It is probably a good idea to choose an on-line shopping website that you have visited before to do this task since you will be used to navigating through the site and using its features and functions. However, if there is no particular website that you can think of then you might want to choose one from the following list:

- buying clothes   www.next.co.uk
- buying sports equipment   www.sportsdirect.com
- buying tickets for events   www.ticketmaster.co.uk
- buying holidays   www.onthebeach.co.uk
- buying mobile phones   www.carphonewarehouse.com

Step 1

Name the website you chose for this task and give its website address.

Step 2

Give a brief description of the purpose of this information system.

Step 3

Describe two of the features and two of the functions of this website.

Step 4

A browser is an item of software that is used to display and navigate websites.

Name a browser that could be used to display the website you selected on a laptop or desktop computer.

State the minimum hardware that would be required to run the browser in terms of:

- the processor clock speed
- the amount of RAM
- the disc storage capacity

Step 5

Describe a connection that would be required to download your chosen website.

Step 6

Suggest one security risk to the website and what precautions can be taken to guard against this risk.

Step 7

You should submit your report with the completed answers for Steps 1 to 6 to your teacher.

JUST A WEE NOTE

In the actual assessment task you are only required to give an example of one feature and one function but giving two for this task will give you more preparation for this learning outcome. Also, make sure that you know the difference between a feature and a function. They are not the same thing!

DON'T FORGET

Just like all of the assessment tasks in this course that require you to produce a report, you do not need to produce a word processed document. You could use a presentation package or webpage editor software to create your report. Use whatever format you feel comfortable with and is suited to your practical skills.

SUMMARY

The report for this unit assessment follows clear steps in a logical order. First of all you describe the purpose, features and functions of the information system. Then you describe the hardware and software requirements to run it. Finally you describe any security risks that the information system is open to and what precautions can be taken against them.

THINGS TO DO AND THINK ABOUT

If your report does not fully meet the requirements of the assessment task then you will be given a re-assessment opportunity. You teacher should specify the areas in which you did not meet the standard and give you advice on how to improve before you are re-assessed. Study the topics "Purpose, Features, Functionality and Users", "Technical Implementation (Hardware, Software, Storage, Connectivity)" and "Security Risks" to prepare for this assessment and any re-assessments.

THE ASSIGNMENT

OUTLINE OF THE ASSIGNMENT

INTRODUCTION

To be successful in this course you have to complete the unit assessments for the software design and development unit and the information system design and development unit.

In addition you have to be successful in an assignment task which is based upon the two course units.

The assignment is a challenging task in which you are required to develop a software solution by analysing a problem, designing and implementing a solution by using appropriate software and then testing and reporting on the solution.

ONLINE ➜

You can find lots more details of course assessment for National 4 courses on the Scottish Qualifications Authority website (www.sqa.org.uk).

THE ASSIGNMENT

You will be given an assignment chosen from a bank of assignments provided by the SQA. Your teacher will choose an assignment that is best suited to your skills and ability.

The purpose of the assignment is to assess your ability to produce a solution to an appropriate computing problem that is based upon the knowledge and skills that you have developed in the two mandatory units. It is set by the SQA and carried out under controlled conditions. This is an open book assessment which means that you can look over programs and information systems that you have previously written to refresh your memory on particular skills that you have forgotten. You can use manuals and textbooks to get more information and extend your skills.

Your teacher is allowed to give you some hints and advice but do not expect him/her to do the assignment for you. You are expected to show your own initiative in this task and to persevere with a problem in the search for a solution. On the other hand don't be frightened to ask your teacher for help if you are completely stuck.

DON'T FORGET ✚

The course assessment will test your knowledge across both units of the National 4 Computing Science course, if you are unsure of any points revise the relevant section in this study guide or ask your teacher for clarification.

The assignment is not just about finding a practical solution at the computer. It involves analysing a problem, the design of a solution, implementing the solution and then testing the solution. You should have picked up the necessary skills to address these stages from the work that you have carried out in the unit assessments. The assignment will give guidance in the form of questions, tasks and prompts that will lead you in clear stages through the assessment.

The Report

A word processed report on the analysis, design, implementation and testing must be provided. Make sure that the report is clear, well presented and free from silly mistakes and spelling and grammatical errors. Have a cover page and appropriate heading and subheading with consistency in the formatting. Page numbers and headers should be inserted together with an index page. Avoid using multiple fonts and styles as the document will appear cluttered and too busy.

People are impressed by appearances so don't let your good practical work down by handing in a messy report that is difficult to read.

Marking

Your assignment is not given a mark out of a total number of marks but is assessed as pass or fail. To pass you need to meet assessment standards in the analysis, design, implementation and testing of your solution.

The assignment is assessed internally by the staff in your school according to guidelines provided by the SQA.

Evidence

You are expected to provide the following evidence for your coursework assignment.

1 The completed solution by providing printouts of the program listing, website files, screenshots of the program interface, and so on.

2 Written documentation of the completion of the various tasks for both parts of the assignment.

3 A short evaluation of the solution.

4 A completed record of progress through the assignment in the form of a log recording daily progress.

> **DON'T FORGET**
>
> Remember the assignment is not assessed on the practical work that you do on the computer alone. Make sure that put the same effort into your analysis, design, testing and report as you do to the implemented solution.

SUMMARY

The assignment is a pass or fail assessment that tests you skills in both the software design and development and the information system design and development units. You must pass this task and also the unit assessment tasks to pass this course.

THINGS TO DO AND THINK ABOUT

Take time over your assignment and make sure that the report is complete and clearly presented. Don't hand in your solution until you are sure that it is completely finished. Your teacher is not allowed to return your assignment for further improvement.

PRACTICE ASSIGNMENT PART A

INTRODUCTION

The assignment task requires you to achieve an assessment standard in a set of learning outcomes.

These are listed below.

OUTCOMES

Outcome 1

Analyse a straight forward problem

Outcome 2

Design a solution to the problem

Outcome 3

Create a program or application as a solution to the problem

Outcome 4

Test and report on the solution to the problem

These standards are met through your solution to a two part assignment given to you by your teacher.

The assignment is meant to be challenging and you are not expected to complete it in a week or two. You will probably be working on your assignment for most of a term in the last year of this course.

The practice assignment given in this book is intended to be of a similar level of difficulty to the assignment you will be given in your own school.

PART A — CHATBOT PROGRAM

A chatbot, (chattering robot) is a computer program that imitates a human conversation. They are used to automate telephone calls, provide voice input for disabled users or just for fun.

◎ TASK

Your task is to create a simple chatbot program that imitates a conversation between a computer and a human user by making the computer appear to respond intelligently to the user's inputs.

The robot asks the user each of the following questions:
Hello, what is your name?
How old are you?
Are you a boy or a girl?
How many brothers do you have?
How many sisters do you have?
Do you think that I am handsome?

The robot must reply intelligently to the user's input with suitable comments. For example the computer should respond differently if the user is young/old or a boy/girl.

Shown below is an illustration of how the conversation might go.

Computer:	Hello I'm Robbie.
	What's your name?
User:	Polly
Computer:	Polly! That's a really nice name.

Computer:	How old are you?
User:	30
Computer:	You're getting on a bit, are you not?
Computer:	Are you a boy or a girl?
User:	Girl
Computer:	That's nice, girls are pretty.
Computer:	How many brothers do you have?
User:	1
Computer:	... and how many sisters do you have?
User:	2
Computer:	4 children. That's a big family.
Computer:	Do you think that I am handsome?
User:	No
Computer:	I think you should reconsider.
Computer:	Do you think that I am handsome?
User:	No
Computer:	I think you should reconsider.
Computer:	Do you think that I am handsome?
User:	Yes
Computer:	Thanks very much. That's very kind of you.
Computer:	Goodbye. See you later.

Stage 1: Analysing the problem

In your own words describe clearly the requirements of the program and any key parts involved in meeting these requirements.

Stage 2: Designing a solution

Design the structure of the program using a structure chart or any other suitable design notation.

Show any inputs/outputs, selection and repetition in your design.

Include a sketch of what the program interface will look like.

Stage 3: Implementing a solution

Select a programming language to create the chatbot program.

Use the programming language to create the program which should match your design.

You can include photographs, screen shots, printouts or other evidence here.

Identify and correct any errors you met as you developed the program.

Stage 4: Testing the solution

Test that your program works correctly and that it gives the correct output for different user inputs.

Record the results of your tests and provide screenshots where appropriate.

Make any corrections or improvements that may be required to the program.

Stage 5: Evaluating the solution

Demonstrate your working solution to your teacher.

Write a short evaluation of the completed solution which includes:

- an explanation of how the program meets the requirements
- any suggestions on how the program could be improved
- any difficulties you encountered in developing the program and a description of your solutions

JUST A WEE NOTE

For the purposes of this program a big family has three or more children and a small family has less than three children (including the user).

DON'T FORGET

The question "Do you think that I am handsome?" should be repeatedly asked by the robot until the user replies with "Yes".

SUMMARY

This is the first of two parts of the practice assignment task. It is based upon the concepts covered in the software design and development unit. It requires you to analyse, design, implement, test and evaluate a solution to a problem using a programming language.

THINGS TO DO AND THINK ABOUT

There is a classic chatbot program called "Eliza" which was created in 1966. Use a search engine to find an on-line version of Eliza and try it out.

PRACTICE ASSIGNMENT PART B

PART B - CHATBOT REVIEWS

A programmer has created a chatbot program which has been evaluated by a group of reviewers.

Each reviewer was given 20 minutes to try out the chatbot and then filled out a form. The form includes the reviewer's details and a rating of the chatbot program as a score out of 10.

Twelve completed forms are shown below.

Unique ID	1
Full name	John Cooper
Sex	M
Test date	12/04/14
Age	20
Score	8
Telephone	07789 324445

Unique ID	2
Full name	Nicola Black
Sex	F
Test date	25/02/14
Age	16
Score	5
Telephone	08892 444553

Unique ID	3
Full name	Alan Lawson
Sex	M
Test date	07/05/14
Age	29
Score	7
Telephone	08879 521333

Unique ID	4
Full name	Sally Wilkins
Sex	F
Test date	30/04/14
Age	83
Score	8
Telephone	07787 509802

Unique ID	5
Full name	David Mullins
Sex	M
Test date	19/02/14
Age	37
Score	9
Telephone	07798 767776

Unique ID	6
Full name	Farah Walters
Sex	F
Test date	01/05/14
Age	13
Score	6
Telephone	07787 003426

Unique ID	7
Full name	Harry Clarkson
Sex	M
Test date	28/04/14
Age	12
Score	8
Telephone	08977 455546

Unique ID	8
Full name	Neil Macdonald
Sex	M
Test date	31/05/14
Age	66
Score	4
Telephone	07789 510977

Unique ID	9
Full name	Rosie Dunbar
Sex	F
Test date	10/04/14
Age	30
Score	10
Telephone	07889 555606

Unique ID	10
Full name	Mark Stirling
Sex	M
Test date	13/04/14
Age	25
Score	3
Telephone	07998 666750

Unique ID	11
Full name	Jacqueline Horn
Sex	F
Test date	23/02/14
Age	21
Score	5
Telephone	08897 311347

Unique ID	12
Full name	Monica Collins
Sex	F
Test date	15/03/14
Age	32
Score	7
Telephone	07788 880910

The programmer wants to keep an information system of the reviewers' data so that the information can be electronically stored and can be used to quickly search for specific reviewers.

The programmer wants to be able to produce a list of all the reviewers who rated the chatbot with a score of more than 8 so that they can be contacted to discuss their reasons for giving a high score.

◎ TASK

Your task is to create a structure to store the information provided which can then be used to produce a list of all the reviewers who rated the chatbot with a score of more than 8.

The list should include the Full name, Score and Telephone information of the selected reviewers.

Stage 1: Analysing the problem

In your own words describe clearly the requirements of the program and any key parts involved in meeting these requirements.

Stage 2: Designing a solution

Use an appropriate design to demonstrate the structure of the information system. You can do this on paper or using software.

Describe here how you will search the information system for the required reviewers.

Include a sketch of what the software interface will look like.

Stage 3: Implementing a solution

Select appropriate software to store the reviewers' information.

Create the software based on your design and enter the data from the reviewers' forms.

Carry out the search to produce the list of the required reviewers.

You can include photographs, screen shots, printouts or other evidence here.

Identify and correct any errors you met as you developed the software.

Stage 4: Testing the solution

Test that your search works and that it can provide you with the correct list of reviewers.

If required, make any corrections or improvements.

Record the results of your tests.

Stage 5: Evaluating the solution

Demonstrate your working solution to your teacher.

Write a short evaluation of the completed solution which includes:

- an explanation of how the software meets the requirements
- any suggestions on how the software could be improved
- any difficulties you encountered in developing the software and a description of your solutions

DON'T FORGET

The information system selected to do this task should be a database. It is very important to get the field types right when creating the record structure of a database. You must decide if each field type is text, number, date, time, graphic or calculated. The telephone number is not a number field because it contains a space!

SUMMARY

This is the second of two parts of the practice assignment task. It is based upon the concepts covered in the information system design and development unit. It requires you to analyse, design, implement, test and evaluate a solution to a problem using an information system.

THINGS TO DO AND THINK ABOUT

This practice task requires a database package as the software solution to the information system design and development part of the assessment. The assignment that you are given in your own school could equally require the use of a website authoring package or a presentation package for this part of the assignment task.

PRACTICE ASSIGNMENT DOCUMENTATION

THE REPORT

The assignment task is based on practical activities but to pass this assessment you must also provide a written report that covers all of the steps you went through to produce your solution. This means that you must carefully check through your report and make sure that you have not missed out any steps in your write-up.

The report must be your own work but you can ask your teacher to check that your report includes all the items listed in the task. However, don't expect your teacher to help you with any input for your report.

> **DON'T FORGET** ✚
>
> This assessment is marked on a pass or fail basis so that if your report does not include any of the steps that are outlined in the instruction sheets then you will not pass.

EVIDENCE

You need to provide evidence of the work that you did in completing the various stages of both parts of the assignment and also provide evidence of your completed working solution. Make sure that you put your name and the date on all pieces of evidence and file them away in a safe place.

Most evidence can be generated electronically with text or drawing tools but if you find that it is difficult to draw a diagram on the computer then there is no problem in creating it by hand.

> **JUST A WEE NOTE**
>
> **Screenshots**
> Evidence for program test runs and the program interface can be achieved by taking copies of the screen through screenshots which can then be pasted into your report document. If you are not sure how to take screenshots on your computer then ask your teacher for advice.

Completed Task Sheets

You must provide a printout of evidence which documents your completion of the various tasks for both parts of the assignment. Your teacher should give you a word processed document which you can use as a template for your write-up.

Completed Solution

You must provide evidence of your completed solution in electronic or paper form.

For the program, this will probably be a printout of the program code and a screenshot of the program interface.

For the information system, this will probably be a printout of database files, webpages or presentation slides.

Computing Science Assignment (National 4)

Progress Diary

Name:	Samantha Higgins

Date	Notes of work done and changes made

RECORD OF PROGRESS

Throughout the assignment task you are required to keep a record of progress of work that you have completed. This is an informal log or diary which can either be in the form of a word processed document or handwritten. It could even be spoken evidence recorded by your teacher in a discussion of your progress or another appropriate format which has been agreed by your teacher.

Your record of progress should be updated regularly. It should give a brief description of what you have done each session and list any changes you have made to your solution as a result of testing and refinement. You should also mention any help that you have been given and list evidence in the form of structure diagrams, design sketches, program listings, test results, screenshots, and so on.

You can ask your teacher to check your record of progress as you progress through your task from stage to stage.

The table below gives an indication of the format of your record of progress. It does not have to take this exact format, but the key thing is to have your name and the date of each entry.

Your teacher may well provide you with a template for your record of progress as a word processing document. This will have the structure and headings in place, to which you will add your own text.

JUST A WEE NOTE

Lots of students forget to fill in their progress diary after each lesson. Put a post it on your folder or computer at the start of each lesson to remind yourself. If you forget to make an entry for a lesson or two you can always fill it in later but don't let your record of progress get too far out of date.

SUMMARY

Your assignment task is not over once you have a working solution on the computer. You must also document the solution by providing a report on each of the stages you carried out, evidence of your solution and a detailed record of work.

THINGS TO DO AND THINK ABOUT

The assignment is an open book assessment. This means that you can look over previous tasks that are similar to the assignment task to help with producing your solution. For example, there may be parts of programs that you have written that perform a function that you are required to do or database files that perform searches along the lines of the assignment.

ANSWERS AND SOLUTIONS

SOFTWARE DESIGN AND DEVELOPMENT: ANSWERS 1

ANSWER 1

(a)   The **binary** number system uses only the digits 1 and 0. These are given the name **bits**.

(b)   A group of **eight** bits is called a byte.

(c)   A Megabyte is the next unit of storage larger than a **Kilobyte**.

(d)   A **Terabyte** is the next unit of storage smaller than a Petabyte.

(e)   ASCII codes are used to store **text** on a computer system.

(f)   The largest positive number that can be stored in a byte is **255**.

ANSWER 2

Convert the following 8 bit binary numbers into decimal.

(a)   4 + 16 = 20   (b)   1 + 2 + 4 + 8 = 15   (c)   2 + 64 = 66

(d)   1 + 4 + 8 + 16 + 32 + 64 = 125

(e)   4 + 128 = 132   (f)   1 + 2 + 128 = 131   (g)   2 + 8 + 32 + 128 = 170

(h)   1 + 2 + 4 + 8 + 16 + 32 + 64 + 128 = 255

ANSWER 3

Convert the following 8 bit binary numbers into decimal.

(a)   00001101   (b)   00010101   (c)   01100001   (d)   10000011

(e)   01111111   (f)   10100000   (g)   11001000   (h)   11111111

ANSWER 4

(a)   Convert both numbers to bytes and then divide.

Hard disc capacity is 2 x 1,099,511,627,776 = 2,199,023,255,552 bytes

USB stick capacity is 32 x 1,073,741,824 = 34,359,738,368 bytes

The number of memory sticks is 2,199,023,255,552 divided by 34,359,738,368

= 64

(b)   Convert both numbers to bytes and then divide.

USB stick capacity is 32 x 1,073,741,824 = 34,359,738,368 bytes

One photo file capacity is 8 x 1,048,576 = 8,388,608 bytes

The number files is 34,359,738,368 divided by 8,388,608

= 4,096 photos.

ANSWER 5

(a)   Program 2 because the instructions are written in binary codes.

(b)   Machine code.

(c)   (i)   8 bits (byte) are used to store single character.

(ii)   The text requires 27 bytes of storage because there are 23 letters, 3 spaces and 1 full stop each of which needs one byte to store its ASCII code.

ANSWER 6

The Integer data type is used to store numbers which are whole numbers and not decimals or fractions. The times for races and running events would store numbers such as 10.2 for the 100 metres and 2.15 metres for the high jump which could not be stored in this data type.

ANSWER 7

The Integer data type can be used to store (a), (c), (e), (f) and (i).

This because these are positive or negative whole numbers the other items can't be stored in an Integer data type because they are either a decimal, a fraction or an items of text.

ANSWER 8

(a) The team names are stored in a String data type and the goals scored by each team are stored in an Integer data type.

(b) The number of corners is stored in an Integer data type.

The number of players sent off is stored in an Integer data type.

The names of players that are booked is stored in a String data type.

There are lots of other variables that can be used as an answer to this question so ask your teacher to check your answers if you are not sure.

ANSWER 9

(a) Dim FormClass as String

Dim Boys as Integer

Dim Girls as Integer

Dim Total as Integer

(b) The FormClass variable is storing an item of text whereas the Boys, Girls and Total variables are storing whole numbers.

ANSWER10

The name of the sport entered by the user is scored in a String data type.

The questions are also items of text and are stored in a String data type.

The answers to the questions (A, B, C or D) are stored in a String data type.

The grading (Excellent, Good, Average, Poor, Very poor) is a String data type.

The score out of ten is a whole number and is therefore stored in an Integer data type.

THINGS TO DO AND THINK ABOUT

The answers given here cover the questions in an appropriate level of depth. There are other possible answers to some of the questions. Ask your teacher if you are not sure of you own answers.

SOFTWARE DESIGN AND DEVELOPMENT: ANSWERS 2

ANSWER 1

(a) The multiply operator (*) can be used to make this instruction more efficient.

TrebleScore = 3 * Score

(b) The power operator (^) can be used to make this instruction more efficient.

CubeVolume = Length ^ 3

ANSWER 2

(a) Area = Length * Breadth

An "x" is not used for multiplying in arithmetic expressions it should be replaced by a "*".

(b) Perimeter = 2 * (Length + Breadth)

The brackets are required to multiply the sum of the Length and the Breadth variables by 2 otherwise only the Length variable is multiplied by two which would not give the correct perimeter.

(c) UnitsUsed = PresentMeterReading - PreviousMeterReading

The variables PresentMeterReading and PreviousMeterReading were the wrong way round.

It should be the present meter reading minus the previous reading to return the number of units that have been used between the two meter readings.

ANSWER 3

The Total variable should be an Integer data type and not a String data type since it is the sum of two dice throws which is a whole number.

The correct instruction is:

Dim Total As Integer

The expression Total = 10 will assign the value 10 to the Total variable and not add 10 to the Total variable.

The correct instruction is:

Total = Total + 10

ANSWER 4

The program sets a Total and a Count variable to zero.

It then repeatedly enters a mark from the keyboard and adds it to the Total and adds 1 to the Count.

It stops the loop when the Count variable reaches 5 and then divides the final value of Total by 5 to display the average mark.

ANSWER 5

The following is a solution in the Visual Basic programming language.

The program could equally well be written in Scratch or another programing language but the same structure would apply.

Dim Name As String

Dim Age As Integer

Name = InputBox("Please enter your name.")

Age = InputBox("Please enter your age.")

If Age >= 60 Then

    MsgBox (Name & " you get a bus pass.")

Else

    MsgBox (Name & " you don't get a bus pass.")

End If

ANSWER 6

The following table shows the value stored in the variables Number1, Number2 and Number3 as the program proceeds through the instructions.

Number1	Number2	Number3
1		
1	2	
1	2	3
4	2	3
4	8	3
4	8	2

ANSWER 7

Program A

The text that is displayed in the message box is "You win."

This is because the variable Total is storing the 7 since Total = Dice1 + Dice2 which is 5 + 2 which makes the If statement true.

Program B

The text that is displayed in the message box is "Don't take hanky."

This is because the variable Dwarf is storing "Dopey" which makes the If statement false so the Else part of the If is executed.

ANSWER 8

(a) The name of the document is stored in a string data type.

The text entered to be displayed in a header is stored in a String data type.

The word count of the document is stored in an Integer data type.

The font size of text is stored in an Integer data type.

(b) An If... construct would be used in the find and replace function. An item of text will be replaced if an item of text in the document matches the text entered by the user to be found and replaced.

(c) A spellcheck would use iteration to loop through each word in the document to check if it matches the words in the word processor's dictionary.

ANSWER 9

(a) Loop A is a fixed loop because it is being repeated a set number of times.

Loop B is a conditional loop because the loop is not being repeated a predetermined number of times but is being repeated until a condition is true.

(b) Loop A is entering a whole number from the user and then outputting the squares of the whole numbers from 1 up to the user's number. If the user entered 6 then the output would be 1, 4, 9, 16, 25, 36.)

Loop B is repeatedly asking the user to enter a PIN number until the user enters 1024.

ANSWER 10

```
Output A
FOR Number FROM 1 TO 5 DO
   SEND [Number * 3] TO DISPLAY
END FOR
```

```
Output B
FOR Number FROM 1 TO 8 DO
   SEND [Number * 3] TO DISPLAY
END FOR
```

```
Output C
FOR Number FROM 1 TO 5 DO
   SEND [Number + 5] TO DISPLAY
END FOR
```

```
Output D
FOR Number FROM 1 TO 7 DO
   SEND [Number ^ 2] TO DISPLAY
END FOR
```

```
Output E
FOR Number FROM 1 TO 5 DO
   SEND [Number ^ 3] TO DISPLAY
END FOR
```

THINGS TO DO AND THINK ABOUT

You will probably be asked to submit your answers to unit assessments in electronic form, so take the time to spellcheck and grammar check your answers. Choose a suitable font and font size so that the text is not difficult to read or is too small or too large.

SOFTWARE DESIGN AND DEVELOPMENT: ANSWERS 3

ANSWER 1

(a) To see if the software can handle data on the boundaries of valid data it should be tested with extreme data.

(b) Exceptional data should be chosen to test that the software can cope with unexpected data without crashing.

(c) Normal data is chosen to test that the software gives correct results for commonplace data which is within the expected range of values.

ANSWER 2

(a) Test data.

Normal data			Extreme data			Exceptional data	
Boys	14		Boys	13		Boys	-15
Girls	12		Girls	13		Girls	Twelve

(b) The normal data has been chosen to see if the program gives correct results with everyday data.

The extreme data has been chosen to see if the program gives correct results with data that is on the boundaries.

The exceptional data has been chosen to see if the program gives correct results with invalid data.

(c) The expected output from each set of test data is:

Normal data   "There are more boys than girls."

Extreme data   "There are the same number of boys and girls."

Exceptional data   "Error message. Please enter the data again."

ANSWER 3

Use meaningful variables names such as Name and PercentageMark instead of X and Y.

Put in some internal commentary to explain what the code is doing.

ANSWER 4

(a) Just because the program gives correct results for 3 grandparents it does not mean that it will necessarily give correct results for other data such as extreme data that lies on the boundaries.

(b) Test data 1   Number of grandparents   4

This test data has been chosen to check if the program operates correctly for data extreme data.

Test data 2   Number of grandparents   two

This test data has been chosen to check that the program does not accept exceptional data that is not valid.

ANSWER 5

(a) The readability of the program would be poor because it is not easy to work out what the variables stand for and so it is difficult to understand the program code.

(b) The program can be made more readable by using meaningful variable names such as Speed and Message instead of Grapefruit and Pomegranate.

ANSWER 6

Two design notations are a structure chart or a flow chart which both give a graphical design of the structure of a program.

(You could also have given pseudocode as an answer to this question which uses structured English to illustrate the design of the program structure.)

ANSWER 7

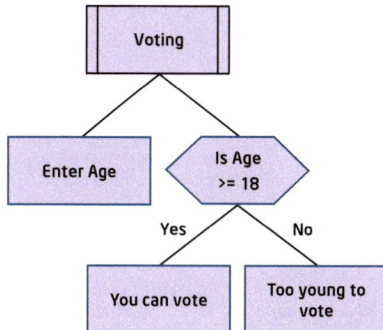

ANSWER 8

Set passes to zero has been corrected to set fails to zero.

The Repeat has been corrected from 50 times to 20 times.

The Is mark > 50 has been corrected to Is mark >= 50.

The passes = 1 has been corrected to passes = passes + 1.

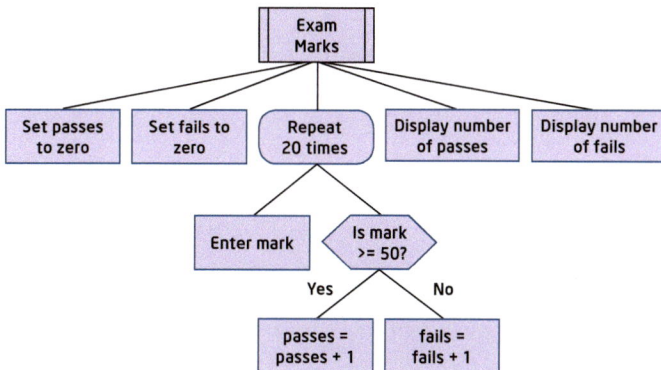

THINGS TO DO AND THINK ABOUT

When answering question make sure that you use any relevant technical terms in your answers. For example use terms such as "internal commentary" as opposed to "notes" or "structure chart" as opposed to "diagram".

ANSWER 9

The structure chart below is a solution to this problem. The entering of the names and ages could be put in a different order. It would not matter if Name1 and Name2 are entered followed by Age1 and Age2 but all of the data must be entered before the decision can be made about who is the oldest brother.

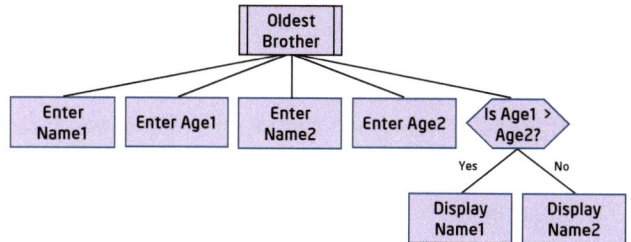

ANSWER 10

The structure chart below is a solution to this problem.

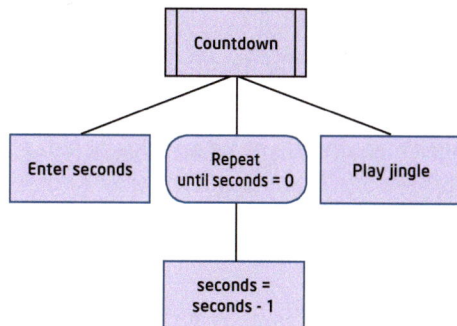

71

SOFTWARE DESIGN AND DEVELOPMENT: SOLUTION TO PRACTICE LEARNING OUTCOME 1

INTRODUCTION

The answers in this spread are of a standard that you would be expected to give in order to pass Learning Outcome 1 in the Software Design and Development unit. To pass this assessment you must be able to answer at least two of the three questions from each set successfully.

Your teacher may ask you to provide internal commentary to explain program code to meet this outcome or to provide written answers to questions as illustrated in this spread.

ANSWERS SET 1

Before giving answers to the questions it is important to explain the purpose of this program.

The program enters the name and age of a dog and then uses a formula to calculate the equivalent age of the dog if it were a human. It then displays a message stating the age of the dog and its age in human years.

Q1(a)   Line 1

A variable called DogName is declared as a String data type which is going to be used to store an item of text.

Line 2

A variable called DogAge is declared as an Integer data type which is going to be used to store a whole number.

Line 4

The variable DogName is assigned the data entered by the user from the keyboard.

Q1(b)   The If... in line 6 checks to see if the DogAge variable is less than 4.

If DogAge is less than 4 then the HumanAge variable is assigned the value of the variable DogAge multiplied by 7.

If the DogAge is not less than 4 then the HumanAge variable is assigned the value of the variable DogAge multiplied by 4 plus 9.

Q1(c)   The variable DogName is stored in the computer's memory as codes for characters in binary form.

JUST A WEE NOTE

In this question it is much better to say "If the DogAge variable is less than 4 then the HumanAge variable is assigned the value of..." rather than "If the dog is under four then it will have a human age of..."

ANSWERS SET 2

Before giving answers to the questions it is important to explain the purpose of this program.

The program enters the name of a vacuum cleaner salesperson and the number of vacuums cleaners sold each of five days in a week. It then calculates the total sales and the salesperson's pay. The pay is £400 but if he/she sells more than 19 vacuum cleaners then an extra £5 is added to his/her pay per vacuum cleaner sold.

Q2(a)   Line 1

A variable called SalesPerson is declared as a String data type which is going to be used to store an item of text.

          Line 2

A variable called Mon is declared as an Integer data type which is going to be used to store a whole number.

          Line 9

   The variable Pay is assigned the value 400.

Q2(b)   The If... in line 18 checks to see if the Total variable is greater than 19.

If Total is more than 19 then the Pay variable is assigned the value of the Pay variable plus the Total variable multiplied by 5.

Q2(c)   The variable Pay is stored in the computer's memory as a binary coded number.

ANSWERS SET 3

Before giving answers to the questions it is important to explain the purpose of this program.

The program repeatedly enters the score on each of two dice throws until a double is thrown. If a target total of 12 (double six) is thrown the player wins a large fluffy teddy bear. If not the player wins a small plastic duck.

Q3(a)   The Do... Loop Until in Lines 6, 7, 8 and 9 repeatedly enters the scores from two dice throws using the keyboard until a double (each dice has the same score) is thrown.

Q3(b)   The variable Target is used to set a score of 12 to be achieved from the sum of the two dice throws.

          If the user makes the Target score then a large fluffy teddy bear is won. If not a small plastic duck is won.

Q3(c)   To win a large fluffy teddy bear if a double 5 or more is thrown Line 5 and Line 12 would need to be changed as shown below.

          Line 5   Target = 10

          Line 12   If Sum >= Target Then

THINGS TO DO AND THINK ABOUT

Print out the code for three programs that you have successfully completed. Go through each line of code and check that you can explain what is happening as each instruction is executed.

SOFTWARE DESIGN AND DEVELOPMENT: SOLUTION TO PRACTICE LEARNING OUTCOME 2

JUST A WEE NOTE

The screen shot above gives test results for the Test 1 set of supplied test data. You should do a similar screenshot for every set of supplied test data. This applies to each of the programming solutions.

INTRODUCTION

This spread gives solutions to the three programming tasks in the Visual Basic programming language. If you are taught programming in different language you should still be able to follow the logic of the instructions and convert the code.

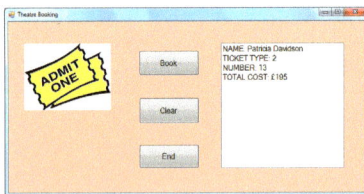

SOLUTION TO PROGRAMMING TASK 1

Interface

Shown below is a screenshot of the program interface with test results for the Test 1 set of supplied test data.

Code

Shown below is the code for the solution.

```
Private Sub Button1_Click(sender As Object, e As
EventArgs) Handles Button1.Click
    'Declare variables
    Dim Name As String
    Dim TicketType As Integer
    Dim NumberofTickets As Integer
    Dim TotalCost As Integer

    'Enter the data from the user
    Name = InputBox("Please enter your name.")
    TicketType = InputBox("Which type of ticket do you
    want? 1-Back stalls, 2-Front stalls, 3-Circle, 4-Box")
    NumberofTickets = InputBox("How many tickets do
    you want?")

    'Calculate the total cost of the tickets
    If TicketType = 1 Then
        TotalCost = 12 * NumberofTickets
    End If
    If TicketType = 2 Then
        TotalCost = 15 * NumberofTickets
    End If
    If TicketType = 3 Then
        TotalCost = 18 * NumberofTickets
    End If
    If TicketType = 4 Then
        TotalCost = 25 * NumberofTickets
    End If

    'Display the results
    ListBox1.Items.Add("NAME: " & Name)
    ListBox1.Items.Add("TICKET TYPE: " & TicketType)
    ListBox1.Items.Add("NUMBER: " &
    NumberofTickets)
    ListBox1.Items.Add("TOTAL COST: £" & TotalCost)
End Sub

Private Sub Button2_Click(sender As Object, e As
EventArgs) Handles Button2.Click
    'Clear the listbox
    ListBox1.Items.Clear()
End Sub

Private Sub Button3_Click(sender As Object, e As
EventArgs) Handles Button3.Click
    'End the program
    End
End Sub
```

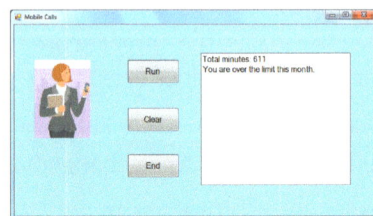

SOLUTION TO PROGRAMMING TASK 2

Interface

Shown below is a screenshot of the program interface with test results for the Test 1 set of supplied test data.

Code

Shown below is the code for the solution.

```
Private Sub Button1_Click(sender As Object, e As
EventArgs) Handles Button1.Click
    'Declare variables
    Dim Week1 As Integer
    Dim Week2 As Integer
```

```
Dim Week3 As Integer
Dim Week4 As Integer
Dim Total As Integer

'Enter the minutes each week
Week1 = InputBox("Please enter the minutes for
week 1.")
Week2 = InputBox("Please enter the minutes for
week 2.")
Week3 = InputBox("Please enter the minutes for
week 3.")
Week4 = InputBox("Please enter the minutes for
week 4.")

'Calculate and display the total number of minutes
Total = Week1 + Week2 + Week3 + Week4
ListBox1.Items.Add("Total minutes: " & Total)

'Display a message if the total minutes is over the
limit or not
If Total > 600 Then
        ListBox1.Items.Add("You are over the limit this
        month.")
    Else
        ListBox1.Items.Add("You are within the limit
        this month.")
    End If
End Sub

Private Sub Button2_Click(sender As Object, e As
EventArgs) Handles Button2.Click
    'Clear the listbox
    ListBox1.Items.Clear()
End Sub

Private Sub Button3_
Click(sender As Object, e As
EventArgs) Handles Button3.
Click
    'End the program
    End
End Sub
```

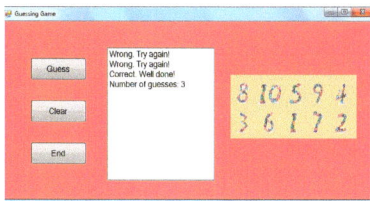

SOLUTION TO PROGRAMMING TASK 3

Interface

Shown below is a screenshot of the program interface with test results for the Test 1 set of supplied test data.

Code

Shown below is the code for the solution.

```
Private Sub Button1_Click(sender As Object, e As
EventArgs) Handles Button1.Click
    'Declare variables
    Dim SecretNumber As Integer
    Dim Guess As Integer
    Dim Count As Integer

    'Set up the secret number
    SecretNumber = 6
    'Set count to zero
    Count = 0

    'Repeatedly enter the user's guess until it is correct
    Do
        Guess = InputBox("Guess a number between 1
        and 10")
        If Guess = SecretNumber Then
            ListBox1.Items.Add("Correct. Well done!")
        Else
            ListBox1.Items.Add("Wrong. Try again!")
        End If
        'Add 1 to the count
        Count = Count + 1
    Loop Until Guess = SecretNumber

    'Display the number of guesses
    ListBox1.Items.Add("Number of guesses: " & Count)
End Sub

Private Sub Button2_Click(sender As Object, e As
EventArgs) Handles Button2.Click
    'Clear the listbox
    ListBox1.Items.Clear()
End Sub

Private Sub Button3_Click(sender As Object, e As
EventArgs) Handles Button3.Click
    'End the program
    End
End Sub
```

THINGS TO DO AND THINK ABOUT

These tasks could have been carried out equally well using the Scratch programming language. Try to solve them with this language. You will need to use scripts from the Control, Variables, Sensing and Operators tabs.

SOFTWARE DESIGN AND DEVELOPMENT: SOLUTION TO PRACTICE LEARNING OUTCOME 3

INTRODUCTION

The report for this practice unit assessment is designed to give you an example of the length and detail that is expected of your own report. The description of variable data types and programming constructs are there to give you an indication of the sort of examples that are required and is not meant to be a complete coverage of the software.

Try and think of other examples of data types, constructs, effects on the environment, and so on that are not included in the report for yourself.

❟	Drizzle	△	Hail
▽	Shower	↖	Thunderstorm
●	Rain	⁝	Heavy rain
✳	Snow	✳	Sleet

SOLUTION TO PRACTICE TASK

National 4	Software Development	Learning Outcome 3

NAME Tracy Turpin

Step 1
Name of the application program
BBC Weather app for Android and iOS
Purpose (What the program is used for)
The BBC Weather app gives the weather forecast for the next 5 days for locations in the UK and international locations which is available on smartphones and tablet computers
Key features
This app is available for Android and iOS operating systems.
It gives 5 day weather forecasts in hourly detail for UK locations and three hourly detail for international locations. Temperature and wind speed are the main values with extra detail including visibility, humidity and pressure.
Settings are available to change the app preferences such as the units used for temperature and wind speed. There is also an accessibility feature which makes the app accessibility to users with poor eyesight by using screen readers via voice over.
Interface
The user interacts with the app by making selections on a touch sensitive screen.
A menu on the top of the screen allows the user to search for different locations to a text box and swiping left and right on the day icons at the bottom of the screen can be used to touch a specific day for its detailed forecast. Pressing on a specific day gives further details of the weather conditions such as humidity, visibility, and so on.

Step 2
Use of variables (String and Integer)
The temperatures are stored in a variable which would be an Integer data type since they are displayed as positive and negative whole numbers.
The wind speeds are stored as Integer data types they are stored as whole numbers.
The towns are stored in variables which are String data types since they are items of text such as "Edinburgh" and "New York".
The days of the week are also stored in a String data type since they are items of text such as "Wed", "Thu", "Fri", and so on.
Use of programming constructs (Ifs and Loops)
The temperatures are displayed with a different coloured background depending upon how hot or cold it is.
An If construct is being used to display a red background if the temperature is hot, a yellow background if the temperature is moderate, a blue background for cold, and so on.
Repetition is used when the temperatures are converted from Centigrade to Fahrenheit. The app will go through each temperature one at a time in a loop to convert it from one unit to another.
Repetition will be used in a similar way to convert the wind speeds from Miles per hour to Kilometres per hour.

Step 3

The impact of the chosen application on the environment or society.

An accurate weather app like this can help to save the energy used for heating and thus reduce the carbon footprint. If you know that the weather is not going to be too cold then you can turn down the central heating settings.

People who can work from home can plan not to travel to work if the weather is forecast to have heavy snow or other bad conditions.

Step 4

Sources

BBC forecast - site search for the BBC weather app

Google play website - site search for the BBC weather app

iTunes website - site search for the BBC weather app

YouTube website - videos for the BBC weather app software

JUST A WEE NOTE

This solution is given in the form of a word processed document. This is fine but remember you could present your findings using a presentation package or by creating a website. Use whatever format you feel comfortable with and is suited to your practical skills.

SUMMARY

The report for this unit assessment follows four clear steps in a logical order. First of all you describe the purpose, features and interface of the program. The second step is to describe the data types and program constructs. The third step is to look wider at the impact on the environment and society. Finally, you should give the sources of websites, magazines, and so on that you used to research the software.

THINGS TO DO AND THINK ABOUT

Choose an app that you use regularly on your mobile phone or tablet computer. Think about how you could produce a similar report for this app by following through the steps in this spread. Some apps are not suitable for this report. For example, if you are finding it hard to find program constructs for one particular app it may be worth considering using another app.

INFORMATION SYSTEM DESIGN AND DEVELOPMENT: ANSWERS 1

ANSWER 1

(a) There are 4 fields in the database. (Student, Sex, Form class, Maths)

(b) The Maths field should be a numeric field type.

Be careful here that you realise that the Form class field would be a text field and not a numeric field. Although the values in the Form class field contain a number it is still not a numeric field because it is not storing a value that could be used in a calculation.

(c) There are 16 records in the database.

ANSWER 2

The Species field should be a Text field.

The Date of Birth field should be a Date field.

The Nutrition field should be a Text field.

The Weight (Kg) field should be a Numeric field.

The Photo field should be a Graphic field.

ANSWER 3

The size of the file = 544 x 96 bytes = 52,224 bytes = 52,224 / 1,024 = 51 Kilobytes.

ANSWER 4

(a) The Stock value (£) field should be a Calculated field.

(b) If the Stock value (£) field was a Numeric field then the value to be entered into this field would need to be worked out manually and then typed in for each of the 1,280 records.

Making this field a Calculated field means that the computer will work out each value automatically from a formula. The formula would be Stock value (£) = Quantity * Price (£).

(c) Other fields to include in this database could be:

A **Size** field. The field type is Numeric.

A **Number of items sold** field. The field type is Numeric.

A **Description** field. The field type is Text.

An **Address of manufacturer** field. The field type is Text.

There are many other possible answers.

ANSWER 5

The records in the database have been sorted on the Score field in ascending (smallest to largest) order.

ANSWER 6

(a)   URL stands for Uniform Resource Locator.

URL is also sometimes known as Universal Resource Locator.

(b)   It is a unique address that is entered into a browser to identify a website.

ANSWER 7

Heather could include videos of swimming events and interviews or sound clips of famous swimmers talking about their careers.

ANSWER 8

(a)   A hyperlink is the feature in a website that provides a link to another site.

(b)   Hyperlinks are usually an item of coloured text or an image in a webpage that the user clicks on to initiate the link.

ANSWER 9

(a)   Most websites contain text, graphics, video and **sound** data.

(b)   **Hyperlinks** are used to provide links to other websites.

(c)   A **URL** is used to specify the address of a website on the Internet.

(d)   A **browser** is a program that is used to display webpages and to navigate around the Internet.

(e)   Most websites have a home page which links to other **webpages**.

(f)   Commonly visited websites can be saved as **bookmarks**.

ANSWER 10

(a)   Sophie could look at the history in her browser which keeps a track of previously visited websites.

(b)   She could save the website as a bookmark or favourite which would allow her to go straight to the website with one click.

THINGS TO DO AND THINK ABOUT

Navigating the Internet is easier if you are fully aware of the navigation features provided by the browser that you regularly use. Choose a browser such as Internet Explorer, Google Chrome or Firefox.

Explore the menus to investigate how to use each of the following aids to navigation:

- look at the history of previously visited websites
- save a website as a favourite/bookmark
- move backwards and forwards between the sites visited in the current session

INFORMATION SYSTEM DESIGN AND DEVELOPMENT: ANSWERS 2

ANSWER 1

(a) Multimedia is a computer system that uses the data types of **text**, graphics, **video** and sound.

(b) Graphics can be captured with a **digital camera** or a **scanner**.

(c) Desk top publishing is a type of software that is used to produce documents that contain text and **graphics** but not video and **sound**

ANSWER 2

(a) VIDEO

(b) CLIPART

(c) MICROPHONE

(d) MUSIC

(e) IMAGE

ANSWER 3

(a) The two devices are a digital camera and a scanner.

There are other possible answers to this question such as a mobile phone.

(b) A digital camera would be best since they can take a variety of images in real life and would not be restricted to scanning in existing photographs which would be the case with a scanner.

ANSWER 4

(a) A function since it involves an action of searching for information.

(b) A function since it involves a process that is applied to the information.

(c) A feature since it is information that the website has and is not part of the functionality of the software.

(d) A function since it describes how the information is used.

(e) A feature since it is information that the booking app has and not how it is used.

ANSWER 5

(a) The purpose of word processing software is to create and edit text and graphics based documents with a range of formatting tools.

(b) The purpose of Twitter is to provide a social networking service that allows members to broadcast short posts (limited to 140 characters) called tweets which can be followed by other users. The tweets can be sent by smartphones, tablets, desktop computers and so on with an Internet connection.

(c) The purpose of a calendar app is to present day, week and month views of calendar dates and allow the user to enter events on dates and times. Reminders and alarm alerts can be set to notify the user.

ANSWER 6

There are lots of answers to this question. Three are given below.

Using pictures and icons to display information and choices rather than text.

Using a touchscreen interface rather than a mouse or a keyboard.

Using colour and artistic fonts to make the interface more attractive and appealing to a young child.

ANSWER 7

(a) RAM loses its contents when the power is switched off. Therefore a backing store device is required to store programs and data files permanently

(b) A solid state device has a faster access speed than a hard disc drive and is more robust which is good for a laptop since it is getting moved about. However it costs more per unit of storage than a hard disc drive.

(c) USB memory stick is probably the best answer. This device has a fairly high capacity (16 Gb is typical) and is robust. It also has a fairly high read/write speed.

Other possible answers are:

CD-RW could also be used. It is cheap and a reasonable capacity of around 700 Mb.

DVD-RW is similar cost to a CD-RW but is better in that it has a higher capacity (over 4GB).

ANSWER 8

A   A laptop computer. She needs the portability of a laptop computer to carry around with her so a desktop is not suitable. A tablet computer is not very easy to type data into compared with a physical keyboard on a laptop so it is not really suitable for typing her books.

B   A tablet is suitable for Alex since it is very small and portable and he does not require a fast keyboard to enter large amounts of data. He can use the touch screen on the tablet to select options and enter small amounts of data.

C   A desktop computer is best for this type of work. This is because Ben needs a large screen display to design the posters and a full scale physical keyboard and mouse to interact with the software. In this situation, portability is not an issue since he would be working in an office or at home.

ANSWER 9

(a)   A stand-alone computer is one that is not connected to any other computer.

(b)   There are several advantages of networking computers these include:

Users can share hardware devices such as printers.

Many users can access the same files. (Multi-user access.)

E-mail can be sent between computers.

Passwords can be used to make data secure.

(c)   Advantage

Wired connections using cables is generally a much faster connection than wireless connections.

Disadvantage

Wired connections fix the computer to one particular spot whereas wireless connections allow computing equipment to be more freely moved around.

ANSWER 10

(a)   An item or hardware is described as **portable** if it is easy to carry around.

(b)   **CD-ROM** and **DVD** are examples of optical storage devices.

(c)   The **operating system** is a large program that manages the hardware and software of a computer.

(d)   **Clock speed** is a measure of the power of a processor.

(e)   The amount of data that a storage device can hold is called its **capacity**.

THINGS TO DO AND THINK ABOUT

You should keep up to date with the specification of computer hardware. Get in the habit of getting hold of computing magazines and familiarise yourself with the capacity, speed and cost of digital cameras, scanners, printers, laptops, and so on.

INFORMATION SYSTEM DESIGN AND DEVELOPMENT: ANSWERS 3

ANSWER 1

(a) New viruses are appearing all of the time and the anti-virus software may not be able to recognise the virus.

(b) A virus performs some damaging action such as deleting files or stopping the computer from starting up once infected.

A worm does not specifically perform a damaging action but brings the system to a halt by replicating itself and clogging up the system.

ANSWER 2

The three words are highlighted in red in the wordsearch below.

W	T	Q	H	C	R	B	S	A	I	K
A	R	L	Z	I	Z	E	S	L	C	J
Q	E	S	W	O	R	M	F	D	F	U
S	Y	D	B	Q	F	G	Y	N	H	W
V	H	Y	C	T	E	S	H	A	Z	Q
B	J	E	D	F	U	X	M	J	G	A
G	I	T	I	R	H	D	N	O	B	B
T	V	F	I	J	B	G	A	R	K	F
H	W	V	I	W	S	E	N	T	R	E
Y	T	B	H	D	P	T	M	U	V	T
E	T	W	N	Y	J	L	I	K	D	S

ANSWER 3

(a) A **virus** is a program that enters a computer and performs some harmful action.

(b) **Hacking** is the process of unlawfully gaining access to private and confidential data.

(c) A **Trojan** is a program that appears to be a gift in order to persuade users to download the program on to their computer where it performs a harmful action.

(d) A **worm** is a harmful program that clogs up computer systems by replicating itself and burying deep down into folders where it is hard to remove.

ANSWER 4

(a) It is likely that Henry's computer has been infected by a virus.

(b) Henry could have installed anti-virus software on his computer which would detect and remove viruses.

ANSWER 5

Just like the Trojan horse in Greek mythology, a Trojan which infects a computer disguises itself as a gift so that it will be accepted by the victim. Once installed on the computer it creates a backdoor that gives malicious users access to the files stored on the computer.

In the Greek myth, soldiers were hiding inside a large wooden horse which came out at night and allowed the Greek army to enter the city of Troy.

ANSWER 6

Computing technology is rapidly improving in performance and complexity so that the current technology very quickly becomes out of date. Consequently, computers are constantly being discarded and replaced with higher specification IT equipment.

Hardware items such as frying pans and kettles have a longer life span because they are fit for purpose for a longer period of time than computing hardware.

ANSWER 7

(a) The use of computing equipment uses electricity which is produced in power stations by burning fossil fuels such as coal and oil. The waste product of this process is the creation of large amounts of carbon dioxide.

(b) The manufacture of computers requires electricity as does the disposal of out of date computers so that both of these processes contribute to the carbon footprint.

(c) Out of date computers are randomly thrown away which pollutes the environment with plastic, glass, steel and toxic chemicals such as mercury, lead and cadmium.

ANSWER 8

(a) Working from home saves time and money by not travelling to and from work.

People have more control over which hours they wish to work and so can manage their time better.

There are lots of other answers to this question.

(b) Working from home is good for the environment because not requiring transport reduces the burning of fossil fuels.

ANSWER 9

Word processing software does not always need to put documents on to paper but a lot of paper will be used up in most organisations by producing printouts.

The hardware of the computer that is required to run the word processing software is using up plastic, glass, steel and chemicals.

ANSWER 10

Tom works on his computer for long hours in his kitchen. He works at the kitchen table and sits on a breakfast stool but recently has begun to complain about his health.

(a) Tom could have a bad back from sitting with a poor posture at his computer for long hours.

He could have headaches from staring at a computer screen.

Typing for long periods of time could cause arthritis of the fingers.

(b) Tom could buy a comfortable and adjustable computer chair.

He could get a screen filter to put over the screen which filters out harmful radiation.

He can buy a wrist rest which puts his wrists in a more comfortable position and makes it easier to type.

THINGS TO DO AND THINK ABOUT

It is common for students to give answers that are too brief and do not give enough description or explanation. The answers in the questions and answers spreads in this book should give you an idea of the length and content of answers that are expected at this level.

INFORMATION SYSTEM DESIGN AND DEVELOPMENT: SOLUTION TO PRACTICE LEARNING OUTCOME 1

INTRODUCTION

This spread gives solutions to the website based assessment task using Serif WebPlus software. If you are taught website development with a different webpage editor you should still be able to follow the logic of the steps and then implement a solution in the software that you use in your school.

Your teacher should have given you practical exercises to get you used to the essential features of a web page editor before giving you an assessment for this learning outcome.

SOLUTION TO WEBSITE TASK

Step 1

I chose Paris, France as my ideal holiday destination.

The software I used to create the website was Serif WebPlus.

Step 2

I created four graphics files in Microsoft Paint by copying and pasting images from the Internet into a Paint document and then saving the file.

The four files are shown below.

> **JUST A WEE NOTE**
>
> There are several web page editors used by schools to do this sort of task. Whichever one you use, make sure that you can insert text, image, video and sound media types. You should also be able to create links between the web pages by inserting a navigation bar.

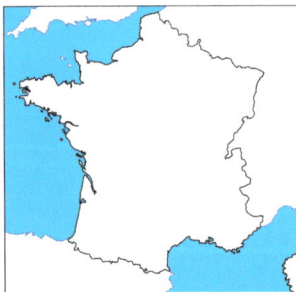
Map image

Hotel image

Attraction image

Weather image

Step 3

Screen shots of the four websites with titles, text articles, images and navigation bars.

I inserted text and images on each of the four pages by selecting the Text Frame and Image icons on the

QuickBuilder Bar and dragging them onto the webpage.

The title text in each webpage is Brush Script MT font, font size 36 and Bold.

For the text articles I used Brush Script MT font, font size 18.

For the background I used red, white and blue to represent the colours of the French flag.

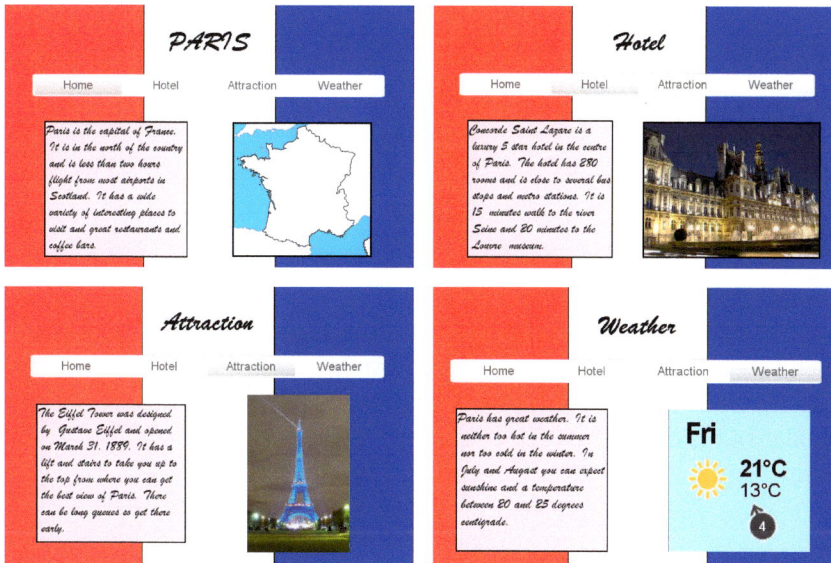

Step 4

I inserted a navigation bar on each of the four pages by selecting the Navigation Bar icon on the QuickBuilder Bar and dragging it onto the webpage.

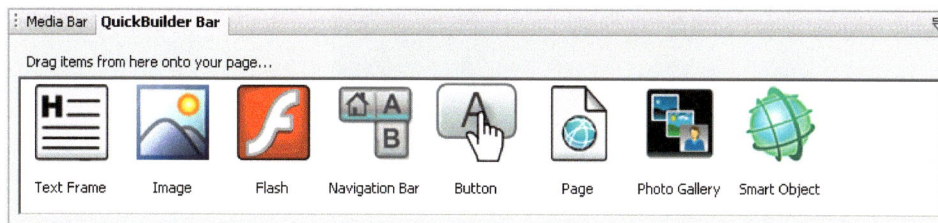

Step 5

Identifying errors involves things such as trying out links to see if they work properly, checking for spelling and grammatical errors, making sure that images display correctly, and so on.

A problem I had was that some of the images were too big for the page and covered up some of the text. I solved this problem by re-positioning the images and resizing them by dragging the handles at the sides of the images.

Another problem that I had was that I did not know how to put a navigation bar on each page. I solved this by searching the on-line help which showed me that I could do this by selecting the Navigation flyout on the toolbar.

SUMMARY

This solution describes the creation of a website made up of four webpages with text and graphics media types and links between the web pages. It also gives advice on identifying errors and how to correct them while performing the task.

THINGS TO DO AND THINK ABOUT

This assessment is an open-book one so you are allowed to refer to websites that you have created previously, notes and on-line help. You can also ask your teacher for guidance on how to proceed, but do not expect your teacher to do the task for you.

INFORMATION SYSTEM DESIGN AND DEVELOPMENT: SOLUTION TO PRACTICE LEARNING OUTCOME 2

INTRODUCTION

This assessment and solution is intended to give you an idea of the level of difficulty and the key content areas that you can expect to be assessed on in your own assessment. It is not intended to be presented as the one and only solution that is acceptable, but simply to give you an idea of the detail and standard of report that is required to pass this learning outcome.

SOLUTION TO REPORT TASK

Step 1

I chose the Ticketmaster website to do this task. The address of the site is www.tickermaster.co.uk

Step 2

The purpose of the Ticketmaster website is to allow visitors to the site to search for and purchase music, sport, theatre tickets and so on from smartphones, tablets, laptops and desktop computers. It is available to all users to buy tickets but is most likely to be used by teenagers and adults.

Step 3

Features	Functions
There is list of events in different categories such as musical and sporting events.	Tickets can be searched for using keywords of the artist's name, sports team or venue.
Ticket prices are given for each event.	Visitors can use the navigation bar to return to the home page from any page in the site.
There are images that are used to advertise each event.	Tickets can be added and removed from a shopping basket before buying the tickets.
Tickets that have just become available are listed separately.	Customers can create an account which can be used to get event recommendations based upon their preferences and to print tickets.

Step 4

The browser I chose is Google Chrome which is available for Windows and Mac computers.

The minimum hardware requirements to run Google Chrome on a laptop or desktop computer are:

Processor	Intel Pentium 4 or later
Amount of RAM	512 MB
Disc storage capacity	350 MB

JUST A WEE NOTE

It is a good idea to set out your report in parts, each with its own subheading. This will make it easier for your teacher to identify which parts of your report respond to the series of tasks that you have been set for this assessment. For example, this report splits the report up into steps.

JUST A WEE NOTE

This assessment only asked you to give two features and two functions of the information system. This solution has given more than that to give you a wider idea of possible answers to this section but you are not expected to give so many in your assessment task in your own school.

Step 5

The ticketmaster website would need an Internet connection to download the website onto a laptop or desktop computer. This could be broadband connection or a wireless connection such as WiFi in a public place such as a library or a college.

Step 6

A security risk to this information system is that it could be infested by harmful software such as a virus or Trojan. A precaution against an attack would be to install anti-virus software.

Another security risk is that the website could be targeted by hackers who want to steal confidential information such as credit card details or use someone's account to buy tickets for themselves. A firewall and regularly changing passwords for users' accounts can help to guard against this type of attack.

> ## SUMMARY
>
> This assessment requires you to research an information system and report on three main aspects of the software. Read over the three spreads Purpose, Features, Functionality and Users, Technical Implementation (Hardware, Software, Storage, Connectivity) and Security Risks. These topics describe the issues that you need to report on to pass this learning outcome.

JUST A WEE NOTE

You are not expected to give a great amount of technical details about the hardware and software requirements of the information system. The main point to make for the software is the operating system that the information system runs on. For the hardware you should mention issues such as the type of devices that the information system runs on and the processor, amount of RAM and disc space required to run it. You can obtain the information from the Internet with a search engine.

THINGS TO DO AND THINK ABOUT

This task could have been done by selecting a different website for Internet shopping such as one used to buy, clothing, sports equipment, holidays or mobile phones. Find a suitable website for some of these other types of products and describe the purpose, features and functions of each information system.

It would also be a good idea to consider how you would do this assessment to report on a website that you use frequently.

THE ASSIGNMENT: SOLUTION TO PRACTICE ASSIGNMENT PART A

INTRODUCTION

The assignment requires a report on the various stages in each of the two parts of the assessment. This spread gives the report for Part A of the task which is a description of the analysis, design, implementation, testing and evaluation of the chatbot program.

REPORT - PART A

Stage 1 (Analysis)

The program is required to simulate a conversation between the computer and the user. The user is asked questions about their name, age, sex, number of brothers and sisters and if the user thinks that the computer is handsome. The computer must respond intelligently to how the user answers each question.

Stage 2 (Design)

A structure diagram illustrating the design of the program code is given in the evidence section of the Solution to Practice Assignment Documentation spread.

Stage 3 (Implementation)

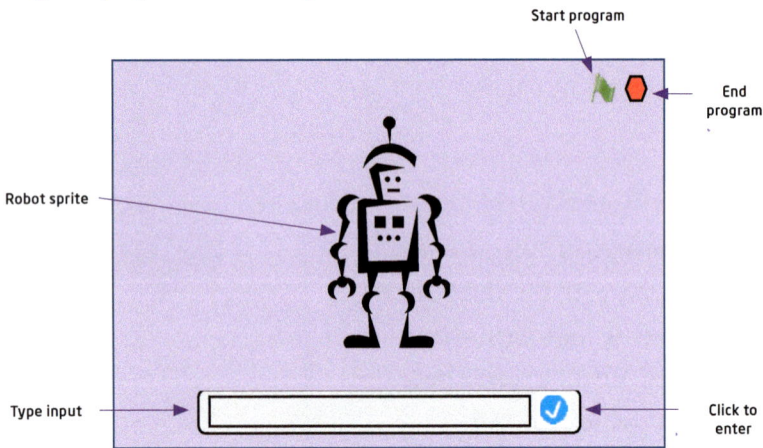

I decided to use the scratch programming language to create my chatbot. The interface is shown above.

Here is a screenshot of the scripts for the Robot sprite.

Stage 4 (Testing)

I tested my chatbot program with normal data to see if it replied correctly to different user inputs.

Each set of test data below was used to test the program and I observed that I got the expected results.

Test Data 1

Name	Age	Sex	Brothers	Sisters	Handsome
Polly	16	Girl	1	0	Yes

Test Data 2

Name	Age	Sex	Brothers	Sisters	Handsome	Handsome
Fred	33	Boy	3	2	No	Yes

I also tested my program with extreme and exceptional test data.

This was done by entering an Age of 22 which lies on the boundary and Brothers and Sisters that gave 3 Children which is also on the boundary.

I also tested for exceptional data by entering numbers of brothers and children that are not possible, such as negatives.

Test Data 3

Brothers	Sisters
1	3

5 children. That's a big family.

Test Data 5

Brothers	Sisters
0	2

3 children. That's a big family.

Test Data 4

Brothers	Sisters
1	0

2 children. That's a fairly small family.

Test Data 6

Brothers	Sisters
-1	-2

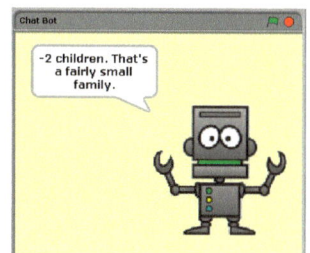
-2 children. That's a fairly small family.

My program worked correctly for normal and extreme data but did not stop me entering exceptional data.

This could be corrected by using a conditional loop to repeatedly enter the brothers and sisters until they are greater than or equal to zero.

Stage 5 (Evaluation)

I demonstrated my completed chatbot program to my teacher who said that it had met the required standard.

My program meets the requirements because it asks the questions I was asked to do and gives an intelligent answer to the user's input. It answers differently for different ages, boys or girls, different numbers of brothers and sisters and keeps asking the user if the robot is handsome until the user's answer is yes.

The program could be improved by getting the robot to ask more questions or by animating the robot to make it more interesting.

I had a problem getting input from the user but I looked through the script tabs and found the Ask script which is used to enter data from the keyboard.

Also, to begin with, I set the Children variable to Brothers + Sisters until I realised that it did not include myself so I changed it to Brothers + Sisters + 1.

JUST A WEE NOTE

This program is fairly readable since it has meaningful variable names such as Name and Age but it could be made more readable if internal commentary had been added to the scripts.

SUMMARY

This report covers a description of the main stages carried out in doing Part A of the assignment. Evidence is also provided in the form of a program listing and screenshots.

THINGS TO DO AND THINK ABOUT

This solution to Part A of the assignment is given with the Scratch programming language. Another language such as Visual Basic or Python would have been equally acceptable for performing this task.

THE ASSIGNMENT: SOLUTION TO PRACTICE ASSIGNMENT PART B

INTRODUCTION

The assignment requires a report on the various stages in each of the two parts of the assessment. This spread gives the report for Part B of the task which is a description of the analysis, design, implementation, testing and evaluation of the database software.

The report is of a high standard but at the same time it is intended to indicate a level that is attainable by a student who carries out and describes clearly each stage of the task.

REPORT - PART B

Stage 1: Analysing the problem

An information system is required to store records containing data on 12 reviewers. Each record has to have data on the full name, sex, test date, age, score and telephone number of a reviewer.

The information system must also be able to produce a list of the reviewers which gave the chatbot game a score of more than 8 so that they can be contacted.

Stage 2: Designing a solution

Design of the structure of a table to store the records.

Field Name	Field Type
ID	Number
Full name	Text
Sex	Text
Test date	Date
Age	Number
Score	Number
Telephone	Text

The search for the reviewers who gave a score of over 8 will be performed by creating a query. The query will use the rule "Score > 8" and display only the fields Full name, Score and Telephone.

Shown below is a sketch of the database software interface.

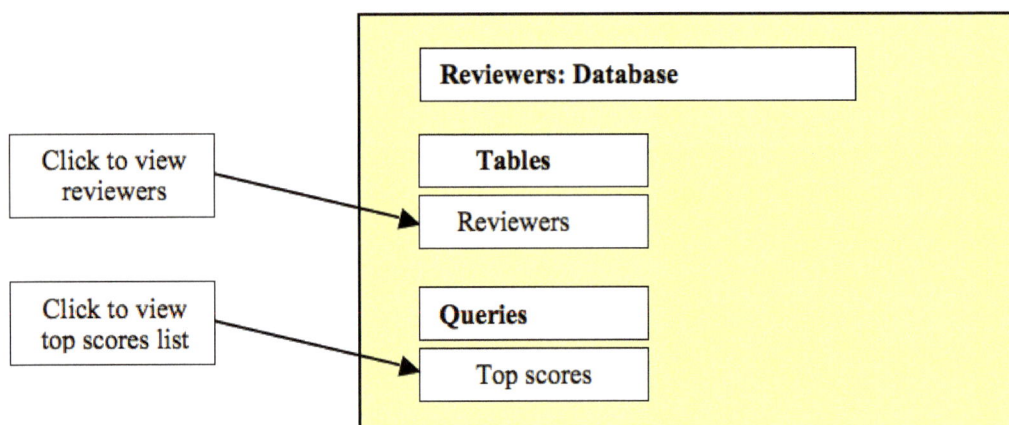

Stage 3: Implementing a solution

I decided to use the Microsoft Access database program to create my information system.

To the right is a screenshot of the table containing the Reviewers' records.

To the right is a screenshot of the design of the query which selects the required records.

Stage 4: Testing the solution

To the right is a screenshot of a test to check that the query selects the required records.

To begin with this query gave me the correct records but it listed all of the fields. I went back to the query design and deleted the fields that were not required and it then gave me the fields that were required.

Stage 5: Evaluating the solution

I demonstrated my completed database to my teacher who said that it had met the required standard.

My database met the requirements because it stored the information in the twelve reviewer records and then produced a list of the reviewers who rated the chatbot with a score of more than 8. The list only displayed the Full name, Score and Telephone fields of the selected reviewers as required.

The database could be improved by adding an image field to display a picture of each reviewer or by sorting the records in the database into alphabetical order on the Score field so as to be able to scroll through the range of scores from low to high.

I had a problem getting the telephone numbers to display properly in the Telephone field because I made it a Number field type but I changed it to a Text field type and it corrected this.

Also, to begin with I had a problem selecting the correct reviewers because I used "<8" for more than 8 until I realised that I should have used ">8".

SUMMARY

This report covers a description of the main stages carried out in doing Part B of the assignment. Evidence is also provided in the form of database printouts and screenshots.

THINGS TO DO AND THINK ABOUT

This solution to Part B of the assignment is given using Microsoft access database software. Another database program such as FileMaker would have been equally acceptable for performing this task.

THE ASSIGNMENT: SOLUTION TO PRACTICE ASSIGNMENT DOCUMENTATION

INTRODUCTION

The "Solution to Practice Assignment Part A" and "Solution to Practice Assignment Part B" spreads cover the write-up of both stages of the assignment.

In addition to this write-up, you must provide a progress diary and evidence of your working solution. This could be done by demonstrating it to your teacher or with printouts or screenshots.

RECORD OF PROGRESS

The progress diary shown below is intended to give you an example of the level of detail and types of content that you are expected to provide in this part of the documentation.

Computing Science Assignment (National 4)
Progress Diary

Name:	Samantha Higgins

Date	Note of work done and changes made
13/01/15	I read the instruction sheets for Part A and described the requirements of the chatbot program.
16/01/15	I made a structure chart for the design of the program and drew a sketch of the program interface.
20/01/15	I showed my design to my teacher who told me to add more detail and then helped me with the types of instructions that I would need to write the program.
23/01/15	I started writing the program and kept testing the code with different types of data as I went along.
27/01/15	I completed the program and tested it with normal, extreme and exceptional data. I also made screen shots of test runs to use as evidence.
30/01/15	I continued testing the code. I had to change Children = Brothers + Sisters to Children = Brothers + Sisters + 1 to add on 1 for the user.
03/02/15	I showed my finished program to my teacher and wrote my evaluation for Part A.
06/02/15	I read over the instruction sheets for Part B and then wrote a short paragraph describing the task in my own words.
10/12/15	I made a design of the database table showing field names and their field types and drew a sketch of the database interface.
13/02/15	I created the database table and entered the data into the records. The telephone numbers did not display correctly so I had to change the field type from a Number field to a Text field.
17/02/15	I created a query to select the required records. To begin with it did not give the right records but I solved the problem by changing < 8 to > 8.
20/02/15	I tested the database and took screen shots of the table data, query design and the records selected by the query.
24/02/15	I noticed that there were errors in some of the data that I had entered into the table so I corrected them and did the screen shots again.
27/02/15	I showed my finished database to my teacher and wrote my evaluation for Part B.
03/03/15	I completed my write-up and checked that I had answered all of the requirements for this task and then handed it in to my teacher.

DON'T FORGET

The progress diary must be completed to pass this assessment. Don't forget about it and try and remember to make an entry after each session when you have been working on the assignment task.

EVIDENCE

Some of the evidence of your solution will have been covered already in the write-up for Part A & Part B but you must make sure that any additional required evidence is included in your report.

This could be sketches of the software interface, designs of database tables, populated database tables, program listings, screenshots of test runs, and so on.

A design of the program has not been covered earlier and so is added to the report in this section.

Program Design

The structure charts below illustrate a design of the program for the questions asked by the chatbot.

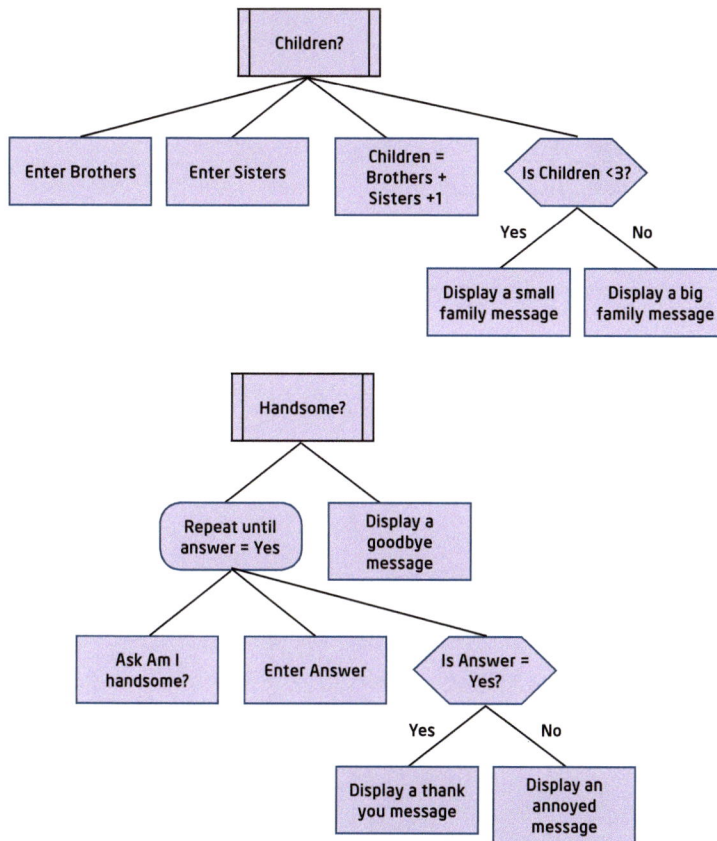

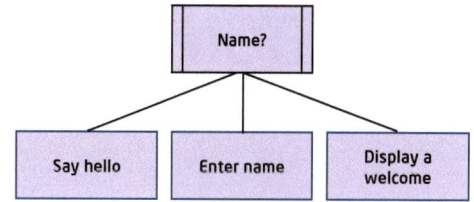

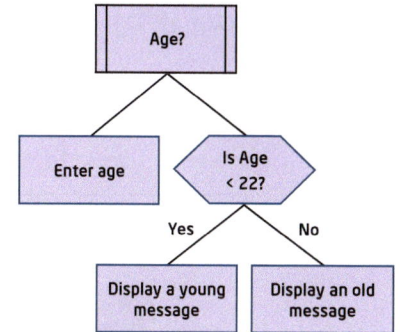

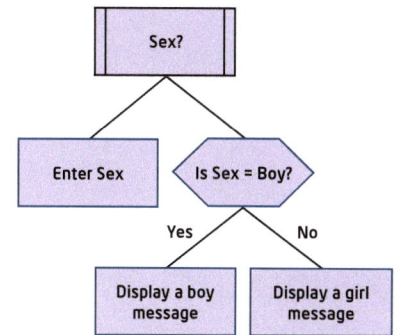

SUMMARY

This topic covers a description of the requirements for the documentation of the assignment in addition to the write-ups for Part A and Part B. There is a sample progress diary and advice on any further evidence that may be required.

THINGS TO DO AND THINK ABOUT

A lot of the documentation of the assignment has been covered earlier in the reports for Part A and Part B. You must also provide a record of progress and attach any evidence such as designs and screenshots that have not been covered in the previous reports.

SOLUTIONS TO TASKS AND COURSE IDEAS

BINARY REPRESENTATIONS: SOLUTION TO THE CROSSWORD (P6)

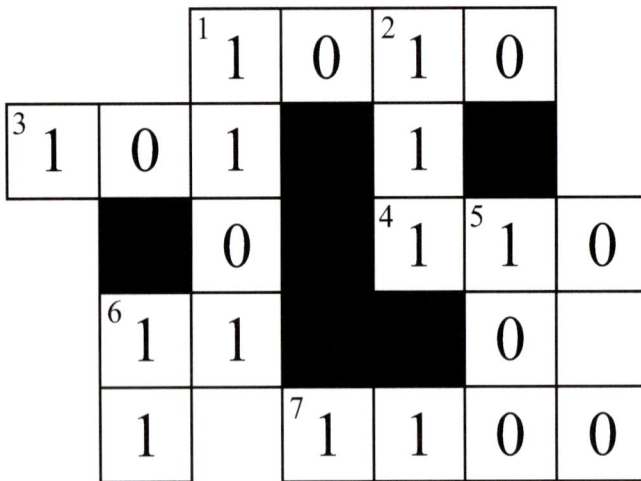

¹1	0	²1	0	
³1	0	1	■	1	■
■	0	■	⁴1	⁵1	0
⁶1	1	■	0	
1	⁷1	1	0	0

DESIGN NOTATIONS: SOLUTION TO COURSE IDEA (P15)

Shown below is a solution to the course idea problem.

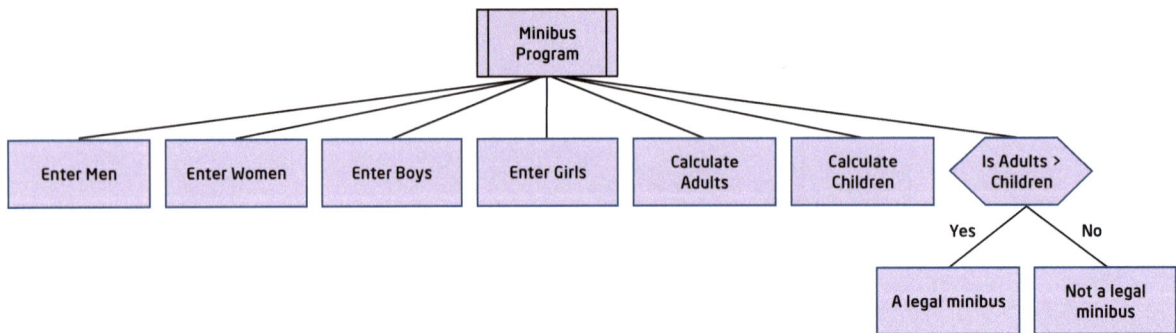

SECURITY RISKS: SOLUTION TO COURSE IDEA (P43)

There is a risk that the bank's system could be infected by a virus, worm or a Trojan. To guard against this risk the network should have security software installed, such as anti-virus software, and other software that can be used to detect and remove malware.

There is also a danger that data could be accessed and even changed by a hacker. The use of strong passwords that are changed regularly can help to reduce this risk.

Anti-virus software
Software that scans a computer system to detect and remove viruses.

Application package
A program that is used to perform a useful function or solve a problem for the user such as word processing, stock control, video editing, and so on.

ASCII
American Standard Code for Information Interchange. A system for storing characters on a computer system using an 8 bit code.

Assignment
The process of assigning a value to a variable.

Binary
A two-digit numerical system which computers use to represent data.

Bit
A binary digit. (1 or a 0)

Bluetooth
A wireless connection that is used over short distances using radio waves.

Blu-Ray
A very high capacity optical disc that is read by a laser with a capacity of 25 Gb.

Browser
A program that is used to display web pages and navigate around the Internet.

Built-in storage device
A device that is built into the computer casing such as an internal hard disc drive.

Byte
A group of 8 bits.

Calculation field
A field whose contents are calculated by a formula using the other fields in a record.

Carbon footprint
A measure of how much carbon dioxide is produced in the making and use of computing equipment.

CD (Compact Disc)
An optical disc that is read by a laser with a capacity of 700 Mb.

Clock speed
A measure of how fast a processor is at executing a program which is measured in GigaHertz (GHz). Current processors have typical speeds of 6 GHz.

Conditional loop
A loop that repeats a set of instructions as often as is necessary until a condition is true.

Conditional statement
A statement that is either True or False.

Connectivity
A term used to describe the link between computers so that they can share data.

Data types
Different kinds of data stored by a variable in a program such as Integer or String.

Database
An organised collection of records.

Database file
An organised collection of records on a particular topic.

Date field
A field that stores a date.

Desktop computer
A computer that is small enough to sit on a desk but is not easily moved around.

Digital camcorder
An input device for video that captures the data as a series of bitmap graphics frames per second.

Digital camera
An input device for graphics that captures millions of dots of light to store an image.

DVD (Digital Versatile Disc)
A high capacity optical disc that is read by a laser with a capacity of 4.7 Gb.

Exceptional data
A set of test data that is chosen to test if the software can deal with unexpected data without crashing.

Expressions
Expressions are used to assign a value to a variable.

External storage device
A device that is outside the computer casing and connected to the computer through some form of connection.

Extreme data
A set of test data that is chosen to test that the software can handle data which lies on the boundaries of possible data.

Features
The features of an information system is what information is being stored.

Field
An item of data in a database record.

Field type
The field type specifies the kind of data that is stored in a field. eg. Text, Numbers, Dates, and so on.

Fixed loop
A loop that repeats a set of instructions a predetermined number of times.

Functions
The functions of an information system are the ways in which the information is used.

Gigabyte (Gb)
A Gigabyte = 2^{30} bytes = 1,073,741,824 bytes.

Graphics field
A field that stores an image.

Graphical object
An image that has been imported into the program interface from a graphic file that has already been created or produced within the program

Hacking
Gaining access to private and confidential data on a computer system.

Hard disk drive
The main storage device of a desktop computer that stores data by using different forms of magnetisation on a disc.

Hardware
The physical parts of a computer such as the keyboard, hard disc drive, and so on.

Hyperlink
A link in an information system to another item within the file or to a document outside the file.

Input device
A device used to enter data into a computer system.

Input validation
The process of repeatedly asking for an item of data to be entered until it is within its possible range of values.

Integer
A data type used for a variable that is storing a positive or negative whole number.

Internal commentary
Comments inserted into a program listing to explain what the instructions are doing.

Internet
A global computer network that consists of LANs and individual computers all connected up together.

Iteration
The process where programs repeat a group of instructions two or more times.

Keyboard
An input device used for entering text into a computer system.

Kilobyte (Kb)
A Kilobyte = 2^{10} bytes = 1,024 bytes.

LAN (Local Area Network)
A computer network that is located in a relatively small area such as a school or an office where the computers are linked with cables or wireless connections.

Laptop computers
A computer that is portable and suitable for use on the go.

Loudspeaker
An output device used to produce sound.

Machine code
The computer's own programming language where instructions and data are written in binary codes.

Magnetic storage device
These devices store data by magnetising the surface of a disc or tape.

Magnetic tape drive
A storage device that stores data by using different forms of magnetisation on a tape.

Main memory
Memory chips in the computer that are used to temporarily store programs while they are being run.

Meaningful variable names
Variable names that relate to the data that the variable is storing.

Megabyte (Mb)
A Megabyte = 2^{20} bytes = 1,048,756 bytes.

Microphone
An input device used to input sound into a computer system.

Monitor
An output device that is used to display the data in the computer.

Mouse
An input device used to move a pointer and select options on the screen.

Networked computer
A computer that is connected to one or more other computers.

Normal data
A set of test data that is chosen to test that the software gives correct results for everyday data.

Numeric field
A field that stores a number.

Operating system
A large program that manages the hardware and software of a computing system.

Optical storage device
These devices store data on a disc which are written to and read from by a laser.

Output device
A device used to show the results of processing on a computer system.

Paperless office
A term used to describe the fact that many organisations now store data electronically as opposed to using paper.

Petabyte (Pb)
A Petabyte = 2^{50} bytes = 1,125,899,906,842,624 bytes.

Portable
The term portable means that an item of hardware such as a tablet computer can be easily carried around.

Printer
An output device that prints data onto paper.

Processor
The microchip in the computer that executes the program instructions.

Program
A set of instructions to solve a problem.

Projector
An output device that uses a bulb to project the computer display onto a large screen.

Purpose
The purpose of an information system means what the information system was created to be used for.

Query
A rule which is used to select records in a database.

RAM (Random Access Memory)
Part of main memory that can be read from and written to.

Readable
Program code that is easily understood by another programmer.

Read-only
A storage device that can be read but never written to with new data.

Record
Data on one person, animal or object in a database that consists of several fields.

Report
A document that presents information retrieved from a database table or query in an attractive format.

Rewritable
A storage device that can be read from and also written to over and over again.

ROM (Read Only Memory)
Part of main memory that can be read from but not written to.

Scanner
An input device that for graphics that scans an image on paper and enters it into a computer system.

Searching
Selecting records in a database according to certain rules based on one or more fields.

Selection
A programming construct where different sets of instructions are chosen to allow the program to make decisions.

Sequencing
A programming construct where the instructions are executed one after another.

Smartphone
A mobile phone that includes functions beyond making calls and texting that are traditionally associated with a computer.

Software
Computer programs such as Windows, Excel, and so on.

Sorting
Arranging the records in a database into ascending or descending order.

Stand-alone computer
A computer that is not connected to any other computer.

Storage device
A device used to keep a permanent copy of program and data files when the computer is switched off.

String
A data type used for a variable that is storing an item of text.

Structure diagram
A method of design that splits a program up into successively smaller, more manageable parts in a hierarchical structure.

Tablet computer
A flat portable computer that is larger than a smartphone and smaller than a laptop which uses a touchscreen for input rather than a physical keyboard.

Terabyte (Tb)
A Terabyte = 2^{40} bytes = 1,099,511,627,776 bytes.

Test data
Sets of data chosen to detect and remove errors in a program.

Text field
A field that stores a string of characters.

Time field
A field that stores a time of day.

Touchscreens
A screen that accepts input by detecting human touch on an electronic grid.

Trojan
Software that masquerades as a legitimate program and creates a backdoor on a computer that gives malicious users access to the files stored on the computer.

URL (Universal Resource Locator)
A unique address that specifies a webpage by the protocol, the domain name, the path to the file and the name of the file.

USB memory stick
A small, portable storage device that stores several Gigabytes of data.

Variable
A label for an item of data that is stored in a program.

Virus
A program that causes damage to a computer system, that can replicate and spread to other computers.

Webpage
A document with multimedia content that is displayed on the Internet using a browser program.

Website
A set of related webpages with navigation between them.

Worm
A program that replicates itself to the extent that it clogs up the system and spreads automatically from computer to computer.